202 Great Cover Letters

202 Great Cover Letters

Michael Betrus

New York   Chicago   San Francisco
Lisbon   London   Madrid   Mexico City   Milan
Montreal   New Delhi   San Juan   Seoul   Singapore
Sydney   Toronto

Copyright © 2008 by McGraw-Hill, Inc. All rights reserved. Printed in the United States of America. Except as permitted under the United States Copyright Act of 1976, no part of this publication may be reproduced or distributed in any form or by any means, or stored in a data base or retrieval system, without prior written permission of the publisher.

1 2 3 4 5 6 7 8 9 0   QPD/QPD   0 9 8 7

ISBN: 978-0-07-149248-5
MHID: 0-07-149248-8

This publication is designed to provide accurate and authoritative information in regard to the subject matter covered. It is sold with the understanding that the publisher is not engaged in rendering legal, accounting, or other professional service. If legal advice or other expert assistance is required, the services of a competent professional person should be sought.
—*From a Declaration of Principles Jointly Adopted by a Committee of the American Bar Association and a Committee of Publishers and Associations*

McGraw-Hill books are available at special discounts to use as premiums and sales promotions, or for use in corporate training programs. For more information, please write to the Director of Special Sales, Professional Publishing, McGraw-Hill, Two Penn Plaza, New York, NY 10121-2298. Or contact your local bookstore.

This book is printed on acid-free paper.

Contents

1

How to Use This Guide

Both hiring managers and career coaches hear it all the time. "Cover letters? Resumes? Those are things of the past. Now it's all about e-mail, job postings, and networking." In my research for this book, I encountered a number of strong-selling books, as well as prominent authors online, stating that resumes and cover letters are passé. Yet the first thing an interested employer nearly *always* requests from a job candidates is a resume.

Somehow, some way, that resume must have a note attached to it: your cover letter.

Some of the candidates I interview earn a six-figure salary, yet they have absolutely horrendous resumes and cannot draft a well-written letter. Many of these letters are littered with typos, sentence fragments, and randomly capitalized words. However, the biggest offense I see time and time again is that most cover letters are not written from the right angle to get that candidate in the door of an employer. It's hard to understand how something that seems so self-evident can be so often overlooked;—it should be as obvious as knowing better than to wear jeans to an interview for the position of vice president at a major corporation.

In contrast, some other letters I've had the pleasure of reading are right on target. Why? It's simple: good letters are written well enough to get them recognized amid a sea of responses. My group has passed up some potentially great candidates with solid pedigrees, but they submitted such poorly written letters or resumes (e-mails, actually) that I couldn't imagine them being capable of sending coherent weekly reports to me.

A great cover letter and resume are important because they constitute the first opportunity for recruiters and hiring managers to see an example of the work you can perform. You are not well represented by a letter that has a typo or is not grammatically correct. Unless they are desperate, recruiters never recommend candidates whose letters and resumes contain such errors. I always decline to meet with anyone who takes so little care in the way they present themselves to a possible employer.

This book provides you with the best concept for cover letters: the consultative sales approach. This principle teaches you to spin your job search around the needs of the employer, rather than your skills or background. It also provides you with many sample letters, letter formats, and guidelines that you can use when crafting that crucial letter or e-mail. It is important to demonstrate your attention to detail and pride in your work when applying for a job—a positive first impression, even if it's on paper, makes all the difference.

I have been involved in this type of work for years. In college, I wrote an article offering fellow college students at Michigan State University some tips on getting hired when they opted not to pursue the on-campus recruiting channel. As an accounting graduate, I had no more real aptitude for being published than anyone else. It's not as much about the extraordinary craft a great writer possesses as it is about attention to detail and pride in your work.

The attention you pay to the details sends a message far beyond that of the words used in your response to a posting or a contact you are making through a colleague. Pay attention to what you write! Because you probably did not get the callbacks, you will never know how many doors might have closed as a result of flawed writing.

2
Writing a Cover Letter

THE STRUCTURE OF A TYPICAL COVER LETTER

I. HEADING

(To include name, address, phone number, fax number, e-mail, etc.)

Patrick D. Dudash
1801 West Cortney Street
West Palm Beach, FL 33409
Phone: (561) 555-1234/Fax: (561) 555-4321
Pdudash@scapenet.net

The heading does not have to include all of the items listed here. Name, address, telephone number, and e-mail address are critical, but fax number is optional. If you include your e-mail address, make sure you check your inbox often. If you list a fax number, make sure you check that as well. And above all, do not use your current employer's fax or e-mail address unless you have their approval.

E-MAIL NOTE: You do not need to use this heading if you are sending an e-mail. Place this information at the signature line in an e-mail.

II. DATE

September 5, 20__

E-MAIL NOTE: You do not need to type in the date, as it will be time-stamped anyway.

III. NAME, TITLE, COMPANY NAME, AND ADDRESS OF RECIPIENT

Ms. Maria Lane, Executive Vice President
PGR Industries, Inc.
1011 Dame Kate
Nashville, TN 23244

The only critical thing here is to make sure you include the company name and the recipient's title, if you know it.

E-MAIL NOTE: Like the heading, this element is not required in an e-mail. However, in the subject line in the e-mail, reference the e-mail. If you are responding to a listing for a marketing manager position, type "Marketing Manager Candidate Betrus" in the subject line, to make it easier for the recipient.

IV. SALUTATION

Dear Ms. Lane:

V. POWER INTRODUCTION

(Attention grabber—generating interest—why this employer)

Over the last few months I've noticed that your firm is moving into consulting with several health-care firms. After speaking with Mike Kiryn, I am aware that you are bidding on the upcoming opening of two new Columbia hospitals. You will no doubt need significant health-care industry expertise to drive this account. The health-care field can become quite complex when you are trying to balance your image as a public entity with the aggressive marketing and sales techniques the field demands.

I have worked in marketing and public relations for nine years, most recently with Humana in Florida. We successfully opened eleven new hospitals over the last six years, and even experienced a storm when we opened the one in Orlando. That hospital opened in the midst of a major citywide controversy over the rising cost of health care, and much criticism was directed our way in the media. Under my direction, Humana successfully overcame that hurdle, and now the Orlando hospital is one of the most successful in the region.

Notice that the first paragraph of this letter informs the prospective employer that the applicant knows the business; the second paragraph then relates the employer's needs to the applicant's background.

VI. PURPOSE OF THE LETTER

After working with Humana for several years, I feel I need a change. I have informed our regional director that I will be relocating to the Northeast and would like to move into the consulting arena, supporting the health-care industry. With fifteen years in key public relations roles in this industry, and having witnessed an explosion in the industry that often resulted in inexperienced managers making fundamental mistakes, I know I possess a wealth of knowledge that I can apply to improving the operations of the right company. As well, I have many key contacts in the industry, but I am not interested in starting up a consulting operation of my own. I can provide a solid lead list to broaden your existing client list.

VII. CRITICAL MESSAGES

I offer your consulting service the following skills:
- *Fifteen years in public relations*
- *Fifteen years in the health-care industry*

- *Expertise in new launches and crisis management*
- *Key contacts within the industry*

IX. CALL TO ACTION

(You must initiate the next steps)

Please expect my telephone call in the next week so that we might set a time to meet and discuss employment possibilities that would serve our mutual interests.

X. CLOSE

Thanks for your consideration. I look forward to meeting with you soon.

Sincerely,
Patrick Dudash

As with any letter, you can use a block-style paragraph format (shown here) or indent the first line. Either is equally acceptable, though the block style is used more frequently in business.

This letter does a comprehensive job of illustrating the way to draw the connection between the applicant's skills and the company's needs. Even in e-mail format, it is effective.

E-MAIL TIPS

- Consider to whom you are sending the e-mail and know the audience; your e-mail alias, your subject line, and your content should all be clear and professional. If not, your e-mail might be ignored and/or deleted as junk or spam.
- Consider your e-mail address as it appears to the reader (this is huge!). I have received e-mails from candidates bearing names/addresses such as "sexything123@ . . ." and "hireme4success@ . . .". These e-mails were subsequently discarded. A proper e-mail address would be something along the lines of your first and last name. For example, my personal e-mail address is betrus@earthlink.net. Save the creativity for your personal e-mails.
- The subject line of your e-mail should be clear and concise. A blank subject line is not a great idea, because it might prompt the recipient to ignore or delete your e-mail. "Read this," "Information," "For your consideration," and similar subject tags are too weak. Consider something like these:
  - Application for Marketing Manager position
  - Follow-up to our meeting of 6/25
- Be aware that e-mail is a form of written communication and it constitutes a real written record. Save and file all e-mails you send and receive. Don't let the convenience of sending an e-mail blind you to the fact that you will be evaluated on your letter and writing abilities. E-mail doesn't reveal your tone, voice, or any hidden message. Choose your words carefully. A well-written e-mail can absolutely impress an employer, and a poorly written one can derail that next step in the process.

Heading —

Patrick D. Dudash

1801 West Cortney Street, West Palm Beach, FL 33409
Phone: (561) 555-1234   Pdudash@scapenet.net

Date —

September 5, 20__

Name, Title, Company, Address of Recipient —

Ms. Maria Lane, Executive Vice President
PGR Industries, Inc.
1011 Dame Kate
Nashville, TN 23244

Salutation —

Dear Ms. Lane:

Power Introduction —

Over the last few months I've noticed that your firm is moving into consulting with several health-care firms. After speaking with Mike Kiryn, I am aware that you are bidding on the upcoming opening of two new Columbia hospitals. You will no doubt need significant health-care industry expertise to drive this account. The health-care field can become quite complex when trying to balance your image as a public entity with the aggressive marketing and sales techniques the field demands.

I have worked in marketing and public relations for nine years, most recently with Humana in Florida. We successfully opened eleven new hospitals over the last six years, and even experienced a storm when we opened the one in Orlando. That hospital opened in the midst of a major citywide controversy over the rising cost of health care, and much criticism was directed our way in the media. Under my direction, Humana successfully overcame that hurdle, and now the Orlando hospital is one of the most successful in the region.

Purpose of the Letter —

After working with Humana for several years, I feel I need a change. I have informed our regional director that I will be relocating to the Northeast and would like to move into the consulting arena, supporting the health-care industry. With fifteen years in key public relations roles in this industry, and having witnessed an explosion in the industry that often resulted in inexperienced managers making fundamental mistakes, I know I possess a wealth of knowledge that I can apply to improving the operations of the right company. As well, I have many key contacts in the industry, but I am not interested in starting up a consulting operation of my own. I can provide a solid lead list to broaden your existing client list.

Critical Messages —

I offer your consulting service the following skills:

- Fifteen years in public relations
- Fifteen years in the health-care industry
- Expertise in new launches and crisis management
- Key contacts within the industry

Call to Action —

Please expect my telephone call in the next week so that we might set a time to meet and discuss employment possibilities that would serve our mutual interests.

Close —

Thanks for your consideration. I look forward to meeting with you soon.

Sincerely,
Patrick Dudash

3

Street-Smart Writing Tips

About five years ago I was in Atlanta shopping at a Barnes and Noble bookstore. After picking up a book unrelated to this genre, I stopped by the career section to see what was on the shelf. Parked at the career section was a young man in his late 20s, and he had a couple of resume and cover letter books in his hand as he sifted over the wide selection on the rack.

I introduced myself, told him I had authored one of the books he held, and asked him if I could speak with him for a few minutes. He looked at me as if I were a little off, so I showed him my ID to validate that I was who I said. Apparently my attire of casual jeans and T-shirt did not lend me much credibility. His name was Derek. We walked over and got a coffee at Starbucks in the bookstore.

Derek told me his approach to using the content in cover letter and resume books. First, he rarely reads the front matter, the instructional part. Second, he wishes that such books would include versions of each letter on CD so he could copy them more easily. Third, he jumps right to the sample letter he needs and copies what he can or leverages the content for ideas. You have to respect a person's candor. And to Derek's credit, he did seem like a bright professional.

I've heard this story over and over, and for that reason I made this book heavier in letter samples than how-to-write instruction. In all likelihood, most people who will read this book are already out of school or ready to get out. Given that, reviewing grammar is beyond the scope of the book. However, good grammar is *so* important! Still, by this point you either know it or you don't. In my experience, proficient grammar has more to do with attention to detail and taking pride in your work than with the gift and craft of a John Grisham or a Dan Brown.

Nevertheless, there are some writing guidelines that you must follow, and this applies whether you are writing a letter or sending an e-mail to a colleague.

Spell-Check

This one is self-explanatory. Please spell-check your letters and resumes; Microsoft Word makes this effortless, but online postings are not so automatic. For online postings, consider drafting your letter in MS Word, where it can be spell-checked, and then copy and paste it to the online application. This is a great tip. As a hiring manager, I do not frequently see misspelled words. What I do see all the time is the improper use of words and verb tenses, and we'll get into that soon.

Shorter Is Better Than Longer

How many times have you received an e-mail and, in your peripheral vision, noticed that it filled the whole screen with text? How interested were you in reading a long dissertation on your computer screen?

Same with me. It is much more appealing to read shorter (read: easily digestible, takes less time) letters and e-mails. That's why for writing resumes we stress having very strong career summaries—to capture the reader's interest in the short opportunity their time and attention span will allow.

A good rule of thumb is to *keep all sentences to 23 or fewer words.*

Strunk and White's *The Elements of Style* is a wonderful resource on writing that many of you already know. It's a very short book, but it provides concise guidance on how to write. Please, if you are unsure how effective your writing is, pick this up and read it. The book is only 100 pages long and costs less than $10.

Short sentences enable you to deliver a clearer message and avoid getting lost in wordy rhetoric. Most people's attention spans are just too short. It takes time and energy to review a resume and cover letter. Your cover letter and resume are crafted solely for the recruiter and hiring manager, and that audience should always be your concern. Thus, make it easier on the readers and feed them small portions. Keep each paragraph to a maximum of five lines in print and four lines in e-mail.

Omit unnecessary and filler words. Consider the following example:

The position for which I am applying is a good fit for my experiences and is a position in which I am likely to be very successful given my past experiences in the industry and in this area of discipline.

Ouch! A real candidate sent this real sentence in a cover letter not long ago. A better way to word this might be:

This position represents a very good mutual fit based on my experiences and accomplishments.

Or:

The marketing manager position requires skills closely aligned with my skills and accomplishments.

With either of these two sentences, the reader gets the message and moves on.

If you follow this guideline for sentence and paragraph length, you will end up with a better document.

Here are some other examples of things to avoid:

- *Well:* In speech this word is used often, but strike it from a letter. Instead of saying, "Well, my biggest accomplishment as the sales director . . . ," simply say, "My biggest accomplishment . . ."
- *Just:* This is another word that clutters your point. Instead of saying, "I just wanted to contact you about . . . ," simply say, "I wanted to contact you about . . ."
- *Basically:* This word creeps into common speech but should not find its way into your letters. Instead of saying, "I basically outperformed my peer directors in achieving the lowest turnover," simply say, "I outperformed my peer directors . . ."
- *Kind of:* This phrase is used as an informal descriptor in speech, but you should eliminate it from your letters. Instead of saying, "Our business was in kind of a struggle with the new competition," simply say, "Our business was in a struggle with the new competition."
- *Like:* This is similar to "kind of"—an informal colloquialism that should not find its way into your letters. Instead of saying, "When my manager was out on leave, I was like the acting manager for three months," simply say ". . . I was the acting manager for three months." (Don't laugh; this happens all the time.)

Avoid Overusing "I"

This can be a difficult habit to break in a cover letter, even if you're not Donald Trump, because you are instinctively writing about yourself and how you align with the target position. Here are some quick tips for avoiding this pitfall:

- Don't begin more than one paragraph with "I."
- Don't use "I" more than twice in any paragraph.
- If you use the consultative approach to writing letters (see Chapter 11), you will focus on the company needs over your own, and that will help you eliminate the overuse of the word "I" in your letters.

If you have already used the word "I" generously in your letter, here is a way to change it up for your closing:

Before: *I will call you Monday.*

After: *Please expect my call Monday morning.*

The first sentence might sound cleaner, but the second puts the focus on the party to whom you are writing rather than yourself.

Common Misuse of Words

This is a true story. I am from Detroit, and one night my son and I were watching the Detroit Tigers, our favorite MLB team. The Tigers were on an eight-game winning streak (for the record, they lost this game), and the television camera panned to a fan's sign that displayed six or seven players' pictures and several images of fire. The sign read: "Their Hot!"

My son commented on how "cool" the sign looked. I laughed and said it was a creative idea but it had a typo. My seven-year-old-beginning-reader said, "But, Daddy, both words are spelled correctly." I explained, much to his confusion, that "their" was spelled correctly but not used in the proper context—a concept that is difficult for a child to grasp but should not be beyond comprehension for adults.

If you use any of the following words in your letters, be sure to check your usage for spelling accuracy.

there, their, and *they're*
- *There* represents a place or time: *I worked there for three years.*
- *Their* is possessive, representing ownership: *Their company benefits are the best in the industry.*
- *They're* is a contraction meaning "they are": *They're hot!*

to and *too*
- *To* is a preposition: *I am going to work at Ford tomorrow.*
- *Too* means "in addition to something" or is used as a descriptor of an extreme: *I will be at the bank and work, too, or I am too late for the meeting.*

your and *you're*: This may be the most frequent error I catch when reviewing letters or e-mails.
- *Your,* like *their,* is a possessive word indicating ownership: *Your company is the industry leader.*
- *You're* is a contraction, short for "you are": *You're the industry leader.*

its and *it's*
- *Its* is a possessive form, like *their* or *your* or *his* or *her*: *Its results were fantastic.*
- *It's* is a contraction for "it is": *It's going to be great working here!*

On second thought, *its* should probably never be used in a cover letter anyway.

Use this Web link for reference, and bookmark it: www.dictionary.com. It's a wonderful resource!

Randomly Capitalized Words

This problem crops up *very* often in resumes and cover letters, as well as in a good sampling of e-mails from any Fortune 500 company. Here are some examples:

My accomplishments as Marketing manager in planning Events, branding, and Advertising provide a strong foundation for success.

Only proper nouns should be capitalized, such as "Ford Motor Company," "Exxon," or "Kleenex." Job titles may be capitalized, but be sure to do so consistently. In the preceding example, my personal preference is not to capitalize the job title. However, if you choose to do so (which is not a glaring error), both "Marketing" and "Manager" should be capitalized. "Events" and "Advertising" should not be capitalized under any circumstance as job descriptors.

If you are unsure about proper capitalization, do not guess. Consult a dictionary, and capitalize only proper nouns such as company names and brand names, and sometimes job titles.

Avoid Alliteration

A former colleague loves to write e-mails using alliteration. Alliterative phrases are often catchy and memorable, and they are frequently used in news headlines, corporate business names, advertising, and as buzzwords. This device is often used to make a phrase stand out to readers, so they can remember it more easily. It is fun, and when you are writing e-mails to send internally, it can be an appropriate technique, lending a lighthearted spirit to the communication.

However, in the majority of cases, a cover letter is *not* the place to flex this kind of creativity, so you should avoid alliteration.

Numbers

If you are using numbers in your letter and their occurrence is frequent, follow this guideline: spell out numbers that can be expressed in one or two words and use figures for other numbers. Above all, be consistent! For example:

> *Six RFPs, four proposals, and two contracts*
> Not: *Six RFPs, 4 proposals, and 3 contracts*

Formatting Suggestions

Here are some suggestions for formatting your letters.

- Maintain margins of one inch on each side of the page and at the top and bottom.
- Keep paragraphs to five lines or fewer.
- Use bullets to punctuate points and break up the formatting for an easier read, but make them a font size or two smaller than the text font size that follows.
- Use a simple font, such as Arial or Garamond, but not a standard-spaced monotype font like Courier. Keep the point size between 10 and 12.
- Make your signature more legible than you might when you sign a check.
- For hard-copy letters and resumes, use a simple paper choice that is better quality than copy paper but free of any "creative" designs or colors.
- Be consistent in line spacing; make sure there is enough white space and the lines are not crowded.
- Avoid abbreviations, such as "amt." for *amount* or "ex." for *example*.
- Use black ink in print, and black or blue (medium or dark) in e-mail.
- In e-mail, include your phone number under your name, and never send an e-mail from your current employer's network or e-mail system.

4
Creating a Solutions-Based Letter

Michelle Bristow is a 31-year-old district sales manager. She has worked in retail management most of her 10-year career. She began as a sales representative, was promoted to store manager for a prominent brand, and then became a district manager over a group of retail stores for a Fortune 500 company.

In 2007 Michelle decided to look for a new position. She had rock-solid credentials and experience and plenty of references. She began circulating her resume and applied online and directly to a few companies that posted district manager-level and director-level opportunities.

After three months of doing this, she had made no real progress. One night she was scanning Monster.com and saw a terrific opportunity. The position was for a regional director of retail sales for a very prominent brand. The posting included the following job description:

This Regional Sales Director position will be responsible for managing and operating a profitable sales territory that satisfies [hiring company's] customer requirements and meets the territory's revenue objectives. You will manage eight district managers and up to 120 retail stores. This position requires the candidate to have successful sales management experience, verifiable, and experience managing a retail operation with over 100 stores and $100 MM in revenue annually. This position will also be responsible for the selection, training, and development of a professional sales staff.

Michelle posted her resume for the position. She also began networking to try to find out if there was someone she could meet at the hiring company. It was a great opportunity, and she needed to make her best effort to connect with this rare senior-level management opportunity.

Following is the cover letter she posted, along with her resume, through the online application system:

Dear Personnel Manager:

Perhaps I am the regional director candidate you are seeking in your advertisement. I'm a very accomplished district manager and am anxious to move to the next level and feel I am ready to take on a director-level role with a major retailer.

I have done a great job as a district manager but there is really nowhere for me to go at my current employer. I am available to meet at your earliest opportunity.

Thanking you most sincerely for your time and consideration.

Cordially,
Michelle Bristow

She never heard anything. After about five days, and not wanting too much time to pass, she called and asked for help with her resume and cover letter. After examining her letter and resume and the advertisement, it was apparent that no connection was made between her experiences and what the company she was applying to was looking for in an applicant. She sent her generic resume and a fairly shallow "me"-oriented letter to the company and did not customize it for the *real* opportunity. She failed to address the needs of the company through her cover letter.

Here are the changes that were made to her cover letter:

Dear [target company name] Management:

After completing much research on the cosmetics specialty retail industry over the last few months, it is apparent that [target company name] holds a unique position in the market. [Target company name] has secured the highest brand equity and premier shopping traffic locations in both malls and boutique retail centers.

In order to meet your aggressive growth goals and in order to complement your brand and locations, you will need a leader who understands your offering, effectively assesses and grows talent, and can ultimately deliver above-plan year-over-year growth.

As a leader with another specialty Fortune 500 retailer today, my accomplishments include number one year-over-year growth, lowest turnover in our division, and highest average volume per store in the division.

My experience is in perfect line with your needs and certainly warrants us further exploring the mutual fit.

Sincerely,
Michelle Bristow

In the end, Michelle received a call when her second letter and resume were sent because they directly mirrored the objectives of the hiring company. Customizing her letter to meet the needs of the company got her through to the next step. This is the primary objective of a letter: piquing the reader's interest and facilitating the next step.

This chapter is designed to get you thinking about factors that motivate the hiring company, and then draws a relationship between their needs and yours, the solution to their problem.

It's Really All About *Them*

In order to develop a solutions-based letter, you need to uncover and understand the needs of the hiring company. What are their hot buttons, their key business drivers that keep their executives up at night? Identify those and position yourself as a contributory solution, and you've really scored.

Research the Company

Researching a company or anything else today is much easier than it was even a decade ago. You can spend 90 minutes on the Internet and learn more than you could in a full day of research the old-fashioned way at the library.

Why Research?

There are several reasons to research the company:

- To understand how it stands financially (no background in finance is required for this).
- To identify their key partners, vendors (companies they buys from), and customers (companies they sell to). This is helpful when you are trying to network to get to key decision makers for referrals. Think of drawing out the six degrees of separation, the shortest connection between you and the company (preferably, the hiring manager).
- To understand the company nomenclature and terminology so that you "speak their language" when you finally meet.
- To discover areas where the business might need your help.

Great Research Tools

Here is a list of tools that can be accessed through the Internet to learn more about your target company:

- *Company Web site*. You must visit the company's Web site, which in all probability it does have. Review its products and news releases first and the rest second. This should give you a good grounding in its business operations and approach.
- *Annual report*. The annual report for a company provides the company's strategic direction, financial standing, and health.
- *Hoovers.com*. Even if you don't have a subscription, terrific data can be gathered by searching for information about the company.
- *Google.com*. This is one of the best search engines. When you get to the search screen, search the company name, the name of the hiring manager, and anything else that might be relevant (such as industry data).

- *Other searches.* Search in Yahoo.com (finance), MSN.com (finance), and Quicken.com.
- *Lexis-Nexis.com.* This is another terrific research tool for uncovering company information.

Now What?

Every time you research or learn something about the company, ask yourself, *So what?* You need to digest the information, interpret it at some level, and determine how you fit into what you're reading to enable the improvement of the business.

Here are some sample *So what?* questions you can ask yourself as you conduct your research:

- Who are the company's major strategic partners, vendors, and customers?
- Who do I know at these companies who can provide me with a referral, a contact name, or a reference to separate me from the pack?
- What are the company's major business units?
- What are the company's key business drivers, key challenges, and areas of pain?
- Who are its major competitors?
- What has happened recently that is of interest (new hires, reorganizations, product launches)?

Why Do This at All?

At home you probably get hit with a lot of direct marketing in the form of junk mail, spam e-mail, and telemarketing calls. These forms of outreach are not specific; they're the same calls the companies make to everyone. How do you feel about that? Right. Now suppose a telemarketer called you and actually knew what your hot buttons were, understood your values, and was presenting something to make your life genuinely easier.

That's the point we want to get you to. Understanding the target company allows you to do the following:

- Understand the company's business and communicate using their language. This will increase your credibility.
- Understand the ways the business needs help and position yourself as a value adder by
  - Helping them make (or save) money
  - Helping them increase profitability
  - Helping them increase the productivity of their assets

Suggestions for Things You Should Research

- The company's major business units
- The company's recent changes in the organizational structure or otherwise
- Major business initiatives
- Major costs and expenses, areas of best revenue (read: most stable for some people), and profit margins
- Key challenges and areas of pain

5

The Hiring Vantage Point

Michael David was interested in a position he saw posted on Monster.com: director of business operations with a national health-care firm. He read the posting, and posted a cover letter and resume. He never heard from the corporation, and his application seemed to fall into the dark hole of cyberspace. Here's what happened to him.

When he posted his cover letter and resume, it, along with many others, was sent electronically to an internal human resources recruiter. That recruiter reviewed a sampling of the cover letters and resumes based on specific criteria posted, such as years of industry experience and years in a relevant discipline. Michael's resume made the first cut. The recruiter did not allow any cover letter/resume ensemble that did not specifically match the desired qualifications to go through. Within an organization, the hiring manager is the customer of the human resources recruiter.

The recruiter thought Michael was qualified enough to make the first cut. The recruiter then forwarded about 10 cover letter/resume ensembles to the senior human resources manager for screening. This layer may not always be in place, but for a director-level position at a large company it is common. The second human resources manager reviewed all 10 resumes. Some really stood out. They had crisp summaries; some were consultative in nature, and in less than one minute the recruiter could determine that the candidates were qualified and worth passing on to the next level. Since the next cut was to include only five candidates for the area vice president to review, the sure things were forwarded. Michael was not a sure thing; he did not make the second cut.

Why? For two reasons. First, he did not adequately customize his letter and resume. Second, he did not make his qualifications and achievements readily understandable to the recruiter. A recruiter is not a line manager or functional manager. The recruiter's screening is usually based on connecting dots between the hiring manager's requirements and the cover letter/resume ensembles the recruiter reviews. In most cases, resumes do get reviewed when you send them in the mail or post them electronically.

What happens next is determined by how well you prepared your cover letter and resume. When you apply online or answer an advertisement, the first objective of the recruiter is to eliminate candidates from the stack and narrow the search for the hiring manager. Fields in the online application that give you the option to select "willing to relocate," "salary range," and "specific discipline" (marketing, sales, engineering) function as screens that help recruiters eliminate you from the pool. Be cognizant of this. You may want to keep the selections specific if you fit the position very closely, or you may want to keep them general. You need to make that decision as you complete the application.

A NEW KIND OF ONLINE ASSESSMENT

One of my clients applied for a general manager position with a top-three non-profit organization. Once the application was complete with a resume posting, the next step was to take a 45-minute online personality assessment test. The eliminator in this process was the personality review. Of course, there is no right or wrong answer to these things, and unless you know the hiring company's criteria and how your answers influence the assessment, you can't trick the system. Nor would you want to. Getting hired under false pretenses is a waste of your time and the company's money.

Employers are struggling more than ever to reduce their workforces to remain competitive in a shrinking global economic marketplace. One of the challenges they are facing is ensuring that they have the right people in the right positions to accomplish more with less. The U.S. government is doing the same thing, according to the outplacement firm Challenger, Gray, and Christmas, where a study revealed that the government sector is starting to pare its workforce.

High-impact management tools such as Six Sigma are being instituted by major corporations on an international scale to do more with less, to increase bottom-line profits through technology optimization (such as scanning your own purchases and checking yourself out at the grocery store without the help of cashiers), cost controls, and efficiency/quality control enhancements. What this means for job seekers is more competition for fewer and fewer top jobs.

Cover letters and resumes, according to a growing number of Fortune 500 human resources professionals, can no longer be long-winded chronological, biographical obituaries that communicate little more than your work history and educational experiences. They must be easy-to-read marketing profiles that sell and promote your value. "Tell us what you can do for us, how you can contribute to our organization, and why you are the best man or woman for the job, and do it in less than 15 seconds," says Eartha Genece, CPCC, of the Newgen Results Group.

With new technology constantly emerging, the vast arrays of communication media are becoming endless. Not unlike a 30-second television or radio commercial, a full-page magazine advertisement, or a headline on the front page of a newspaper, we have only a few seconds to capture the attention of the readers to get them to want to read on!

WHAT TO AVOID

The following are seven mistakes made in letters that employers claim hinder a job seeker's chances of securing an interview and eventually a job.

1. Lack of Organization

You must organize the letter and the information contained within it so that the reader is able to read the important information first. The important information is information that communicates your value—your ability to contribute in a meaningful way—in less than 15 seconds. A good question to ask when organizing your letter is, "What do I need to communicate to the reader that will ignite interest in me so that he or she will want to read the rest of the letter and click on the resume with interest and then invite me into the interview?"

2. Information That Is Too General

What does "good communication skills" mean? Does it mean you can give a speech to 2,500 people, negotiate an arms deal, or write a best-selling book?

What does "problem-solving skills" mean? What is a "people person"? As you can see from these examples, far too many job seekers are using the same common phrases, words, and concepts in letters and resumes that look like those of most other job candidates and don't specify exactly how the concepts can benefit the prospective employer. If applicants used the same words and phrases in their resumes, it would be like watching a NASCAR race with 14 cars that looked exactly alike—you'd never know who was who!

When writing your letters and resume, instead of saying you have good communications skills, say that you have high-impact negotiating or presentation skills, solid public speaking abilities, or strong writing and editing skills backed up like the examples in Chapter 13 of this book. Instead of saying you are a problem solver, state that you can troubleshoot technical equipment, resolve human conflicts in the workplace, or resolve customer service issues professionally and effectively.

3. Lack of Achievements

A cover letter/resume ensemble without achievements is like a report card without grades. It's not what you have done that is important but how well you have done it. If 25 students in a class take math, English, science, history, and social studies, what differentiates them?

Grades = results! The message in your cover letters and resume is like a report card: what did you do, and how did you do it? Achievements come in two forms: qualitative and quantitative.

Quantitative achievements are specific achievements, for example:

- Increased sales 23 percent year over year
- Improved customer service levels from 91.3 percent to 98.7 percent
- Enhanced market share from 21 percent to 31 percent
- Increased profits $1.3 million a year, or $.82 per share

Qualitative achievements are nonmeasurable results, but they are accomplishments just the same:

- Significantly increased sales
- Dramatically improved the level of customer service
- Decreased expenses while improving market share
- Improved efficiency and productivity while lowering personnel turnover

Remember, an ensemble without achievements is like a report card without grades, and when you look like everyone else, you can't possibly get noticed. When it comes to standing out, *conformity is a recipe for disaster*.

4. Resumes Not Written for Both People and Technology

Today many larger corporations are using computers with keyword software to read the plethora of resumes sent to them by job seekers. Most electronic resumes are sent as e-mail attachments, and the integrity of the formatted resume can be retained because the improved software can read the document with the enhancements included. *Note: Your resume must be compatible with Microsoft Word.*

The goal is to write an effective ensemble that includes all the relevant industry keywords. Keywords are descriptive words, usually nouns that are associated with specific disciplines or industries. Keywords (refer to *2,500 Keywords to Get You Hired*, McGraw-Hill, 2003) play an integral role in two areas of the resume-screening process. One is the human element—the eyes-only element—in which hiring and nonhiring managers are screening resumes for words and phrases that match their criteria.

The second is the computer search, where software is developed to seek out keywords that also match the criteria of employers. When you are writing a resume, industry keywords need to be identified and used throughout the resume.

5. Cover Letters That Tell but Don't Sell

Your cover letters and resume should not be long-winded biographies. Rather, they must communicate what you can do for the company and how you can improve its economics—its goals and objectives. You have never seen an advertisement for Coca-Cola providing you with the complete history of Coca-Cola. General Motors doesn't provide a year-by-year historical account of the company when selling automobiles. Employers don't want to know about your history without that connection. What they want to know is what your value is to them: how you can benefit them and how they can profit from you!

Your work experience, education, and functional strengths are relevant only to the extent that they provide evidence of how you can help the company. You are using your cover letter/resume ensemble in what we call the "job market," and the job market is no different from the marketplace in general in that there is stiff competition.

To attract the outstanding jobs, you must stand out on your resume and subsequently in the interview. Your job is to sell your value, not relate your historical biography.

6. Resumes That Contain No Value-Added Messages

This mistake can often be the difference between victory and defeat. A value-added message shows how a candidate can add value to an organization in a way that is not specific to the hiring company. Companies want to know what you can do for them and the types of contributions you'll make. If a company is seeking a sales professional and the top three candidates all have about the same education, work experience, achievements, and credentials and are all well liked, what will tilt the scale in one candidate's favor? Often it's that *value-added* dimension that one of the candidates brings to the table.

If one candidate speaks English, Spanish, and French fluently, that value-added dimension may be helpful in opening new markets that use those languages, and thus that person will be offered the job. If a licensed esthetician is also an effective salesperson and can bring in new business as well as do facials and spa treatments, that added dimension would be instrumental in giving that person an advantage over other estheticians who do only treatment work. As you think about identifying the value you bring to your next job, also think about what value-added aspects you bring to the job that would benefit the company or organization and differentiate you from the competition.

7. Resumes That Are Riddled with Typos and Grammatical Errors

Yes, this still occurs on a regular basis and remains a major irritant for those who read resumes. Spell-check won't catch a misused tense ("achieved" instead of "achieve"), a misused word ("in" instead of "if"), or a wrong date (1989 instead of 1998). When you are finished writing your resume, select a handful of qualified people you know and trust to read and proofread it. One little typo can be disastrous in your effort to land the interview and win the job. Have your letters and resume proofed by competent people so that you don't put yourself out of contention for top jobs.

6

Broadcast Letters

The broadcast letter is a hybrid between a resume and a cover letter. Candidates use it when they do not wish to send their full resume.

There are many instances when a broadcast letter will be more effective initially in generating interest in a candidate. The broadcast letter looks more like a letter than a resume, so the reader may be apt to give it a bit more attention. This is especially true when a screening authority (secretary or administrative assistant) is screening mail or e-mails. The screener is more likely to pass on a "letter" to the boss but might more readily redirect a "resume" to personnel or human resources.

Suppose you are employed but do not want to take any chances in having your current employer find out you are looking for a job. Certainly you will not want to send out a resume that names your current employer. This would be a good time to consider creating a broadcast letter.

UNDERSTANDING YOUR TARGETED READER

As a general rule, broadcast letters are sent to hiring managers, not recruiters (internal or external).

Because you may not be writing for a specific job opening, you do not need to reference the letter to a specific position or even job reference number. However, in the subject line of the e-mail, the most common way to communicate, you can list your specialty or the job title you are hoping to fill. This might be

"Marketing Manager," or "Director of Operations," or "Senior Sales Manager." Whatever the appropriate title for you, include it.

The first paragraph is what separates the broadcast cover letter from the typical cover letter. You're really broadcasting your interest and accomplishments, so that part of the approach is different from the more direct approach. Probably the easiest distinction for the marketing folks to grasp in a resume is a call to action, where a broadcast letter is more about branding.

The second paragraph addresses the particular needs, concerns, missions, and goals of the company, much like the consultative approach discussed throughout this book. Your potential contribution, that connection to the company mission, is the point you cannot lose.

In the closing paragraph, end with a call to action—an action you need to control. Be direct about when you plan to follow up.

Debbie Davis
110 Cumberland Way, Atlanta, GA 30303

February 5, 20__

Doug Matheson
Chiat Day
1 Boca Way
Boca Raton, FL 33678

Dear Mr. Matheson:

In today's highly competitive market, companies need an advertising message to differentiate themselves and facilitate increased market penetration. I am writing you because your company may need someone with my experience. I invite you to consider my recent accomplishments:

o Ranked #1 among RCA's six global regions, 2003, 2004, and 2005. Grew key account base by 72% in first year, representing new revenues of $48 million.

o Developed concepts and designs for clients in the film, theater, nonprofit, and fashion industries. Designed special promotional material, direct-mail brochures, press kits, and corporate identities. Produced exceptional-quality work for clients on a tight budget and a tight deadline.

o Reputation for completing projects on time and in budget with solutions focused on meeting marketing and promotional metrics, articulating strategic communications objectives, and maximizing production efficiencies.

o Polished interpersonal and communications skills, with public speaking and presentation abilities. Wide range of computer systems and software knowledge and experience.

o Manage an advertising operations support team of eight with a sales budget of $58 million.

I would welcome the opportunity to speak with you regarding any opportunities you may have now or in the future. Should you agree that my background is a good match for your requirements, please contact me at your earliest convenience.

Sincerely,

Debbie Davis

Dawn B.W. McCarter

400 Las Colinas, Irving, TX 77777

October 24, 20__

Sal Todaro
Marriott International
1400 Michigan Avenue
Chicago, IL 00000

Dear Mr. Todaro:

Thank you so much for speaking with me regarding the general manager position you are trying to fill for your property in Madison. I am looking forward to meeting you and discussing the possibilities. Based on the description of the position and the information you shared, it does look like a potentially good mutual fit, certainly one worth exploring for both of us.

Following are a few career highlights and accomplishments:

- Fifteen years' experience in hotel management and operations.

- Responsible for the creation of all service concepts, training, and hiring of all employees at a Radisson International in another major college town. Responsible for overseeing all aspects of the Rooms Division operation. Also in charge of initiating and maintaining vendor relations.

- Managed the operation of a 285-room full-service convention hotel with 31,000 square feet of meeting space. Since my arrival, increased market share from 79% to 124%, REVPAR by 28%, and rooms sold by 25%.

- Exceeded 90% of guest satisfaction score goals in the opening year of business. Exceeded 95% of Rooms Division employee satisfaction criteria in first year of operation. Internally rated the third highest hotel within the U.S. in occupancy.

- Oversee 617-room full-service convention hotel with 58,000 square feet of meeting space. In the process of reorganizing the management structure. Redeploying the sales effort to increase REVPAR and market share.

I am looking forward to meeting with you face-to-face to discuss this opportunity in more detail.

Sincerely,

Dawn B.W. McCarter

Oren Laufter
400 Las Colinas, Irving, TX 77777

July 2, 20__

Eileen Statsworthy
MCNA
202 Woodward Avenue
Detroit, MI 48221

Dear Ms. Statsworthy:

Today's leaders in the commercial financial industry need to understand both how to create profits in their business and how their business enables others to create profits. If you need a visionary senior-level executive who has proven to be able to accomplish both of these things, we should get together to discuss options.

The following accomplishments reflect what I can bring to MCNA:

- Reduced retail delinquency from 4.45% in 2003 to 1.79% in 2005.

- Assumed additional responsibility of servicing all commercial collections deemed as "workout status." Accepted the responsibility of managing the bank's Other Retail Estate Owned (ORE). Reduced ORE from $1.1 million to $700,000.

- Centralized the Indirect Lending operation into a single location servicing 46 auto dealers in the Metro-East area. With two underwriters and a clerical staff of four, processed more than 1,000 applications each month. Purchased $11 million in auto loan paper in the first three months of 1993 for a net gain of $3 million.

- Centralized Direct Lending operation into a single department processing approximately 200 direct loan applications per month. Provided a centralized approval process for Central Bank's 11 locations.

- Successfully organized and set up Secondary Mortgage Department for Central Bank in 1999. Originally started this effort as the sole underwriter for FNMA. Formulated a staff that grew the department to $12 million in FNMA loans and serviced the direct real estate loans totaling $60 million. FNMA delinquency was zero when I left Central Bank.

- Manage operations, personnel, budget, profit planning, and audit and compliance for branch with assets up to $19 million. Proven ability to achieve success given difficult situations. Turned around Mason branch within three months, bringing branch within audit compliance. Maintained excellent audit ratings. Effectively managed branch throughout merger process.

- Strong leadership skills with the ability to generate enthusiasm among staff. Supervise, develop, and direct staff of seven.

Ms. Statsworthy, if you are seeking an executive who can step in with a short learning curve and effect change, we really should get together to explore this further.

Sincerely,

Oren Laufter

27

HENRY ALCORN

14 Park Avenue • New York, New York 00000 • (212) 555-5555 • ha@qol.com

August 1, 20__

Greg Hollister
Hollister and Associates
101 Avenue of the Americas
New York, NY 00000

Dear Mr. Hollister:

Thank you for reaching out to me in your search for a new CEO for the MVNO. I am the founder and operations leader of this company aimed at the developing market for mobile broadband wireless access. Here I performed all financial planning and raised seed funding from Chase and supporting founding team members, defined vertical markets, and constructed strategic marketing plans for market penetration. We modeled complete network infrastructure market by market and met our rollout and sales expectations ahead of schedule, due in large part to the highly talented professionals we placed in key roles. Here are some other brief highlights:

- Built unique trial system consisting of broadband connectivity structure, VPN, and ClicktoMeet™ video services plus complete network model for all markets.
- Played key role in negotiation of corporate acquisition of privately held company (Centennial) by Davidson Corporation.
- Smoothed transition from private to public company while continuing to achieve revenue and profitability growth, increased levels of production, and customer satisfaction.
- More than doubled revenues from $21 million to $52 million within three years.
- Brought to market the family of CATZ brand radios that operated in the ISM band of frequencies for unlicensed end-user applications using cutting-edge DSSS technology.
- Successfully brought division through several periods of expansion and contraction without loss of profitability and with zero reduction in labor force.

I am confident in my ability to replicate this success through good planning and the ability to raise financing and select strong functional leadership.

Sincerely,

Henry Alcorn

Jennifer Johnson

3 Dallas Way
Grapevine, TX 75555
(972) 555-5555

January 8, 20__

Ms. Tammy Cancela
430 Houston Way
Houston, TX 78444

Dear Ms. Cancela:

Thank you for speaking with me this week. I am very excited about the prospect of joining your teaching staff, to challenge students to learn and prepare them for their future. It is a highly rewarding experience for us as teachers to watch our students grow and evolve into adulthood. Below are some of my career highlights and qualifications for your reference.

Curriculum Development and Instruction

- Assisted in the development, validation, and enhancement of curricula. Introduced hands-on tools (e.g., computer technology, outside classroom activities) to improve classroom interest and retention.
- Taught a full academic curriculum (reading, writing, communications, mathematics, social science) to children ages 7 to 13.
- Designed and implemented customized teaching programs to allow emotionally, physically, and learning disabled students to be mainstreamed into the classroom.
- Launched a highly successful peer-tutoring program designed to improve interaction between upper-level and younger students while fostering communication and mentoring skills at all levels.

Administration and Special Activities

- Appointed vice principal with responsibility for diverse functions including faculty recruitment and scheduling, curriculum development, discipline, parent/community affairs, and special events planning.
- Prepared documentation for recertification by the National Accreditation of Schools Committee as a member of a cross-functional faculty/administration committee.
- Provided classroom training, performance evaluation, and motivation as a mentor to student teachers completing college requirements for an education degree.

I will forward you my academic credentials and portfolio next week. I will contact you at the end of the month to arrange the next steps. Once again, thank you for considering my candidacy. I look forward to becoming a member of your fine staff.

Sincerely,

Jennifer Johnson

Jonathan Diego

1 Main Street, Atlanta, GA 33333 jd@rrr.com

May 18, 20__

Mr. Steven Hunt
Ford Creative
Two Culver Place
Miami, FL 33333

Dear Mr. Hunt:

As an advertising executive with Chiat Day for the past six years, I have developed an impeccable record of acquiring key accounts and retaining them through skilled relationship management.

Key Strengths

* Acumen for developing solutions
* Presentation and graphic arts expertise
* Client acquisition and retention

* Strategic research of client needs
* Development of key ideas
* Team leadership within agency

Past Employment

Chiat Day, San Francisco   **Client Executive**
Target Scope, Dallas   **Account Team Leader**
Fletcher Martin, Atlanta   **Account Executive**

I will call you next Tuesday to arrange a meeting where we can discuss the direction Ford is taking and a potential fit for future business. I will also bring my portfolio and offer references from clients to support the acquisition and retention skills that I demonstrated.

Thanks in advance for your time and consideration.

Sincerely,

Jonathan Diego

Tom Morgan
Denver, CO
tmorgan@ert.com

March 20, 20__

Elena Dayton
Clements Community Center
14 Elm Street
Lakewood, CO 80000

Dear Ms. Dayton:

Alanis Montgomery shared with me some of your wonderful accomplishments at CCC, including the turnaround at the facility and the increased membership over the past two years.

Alanis has known me for several years and thought it would be great if we got together to discuss ideas. I set up the children's development program at the YCC in Colorado Springs, and the program is considered one of the best in the country. I would like to explore working with you to build CCC into a center by which all others in the state are measured. I will call you at the end of next week, but here are a few highlights of my career:

Achievements

- Experienced as a campaign consultant in feasibility studies, volunteer development, and seven-figure investment development.
- Managed significant chamber campaigns, all under budget and over goal. Oversaw all systems and operational issues with clients and my team.
- Built on existing volunteer development to increase over 50%.
- Successfully conceived and oversaw the various fund-raising campaigns that have enabled us to operate in the black since inception. Successfully developed newsletters (current circulation 4,000), database, internal documentation, and externally focused literature.
- Raised over $4.2 million in the past five years.
- Five-year consistent record of attaining projected fund-raising targets.

Education

Master of Arts in Philosophy   Colorado State University
Bachelor of Arts in History   University of Arizona

I will call you soon to discuss some possibilities. Even if you do not have a specific position right now, I'd like to establish the contact and discuss past experiences in this business. Thanks, Elena. I'm looking forward to speaking with you soon.

Sincerely,

Tom Morgan

Melissa Sumner

1 Moon Drive, Houston, TX 77777 832.555.1111 ms@tygle.net

March 1, 20___

Helen Kramer
David Weekly Homes
I King Arthur, Lewisville, TX 75056

Dear Ms. Kramer:

I have noticed with envy the rapid expansion of your new development in North Dallas. This is indeed a growing area, and Castle Hills is uniquely equipped to take advantage of the expansion to the north part of town.

I would like to interview for the builder position open for phase three in the development, leading the various trades and overall construction process.

I offer you the following:

- ❑ Eleven years' experience as crew leader for residential construction, rough carpentry.
- ❑ Directed a crew of ten people on the job site in one of Dallas's largest housing developments.
- ❑ Built loyal client base through personal attention, quality service, and consistency.
- ❑ Established reputation for excellence within local communities.
- ❑ Demonstrated ability to work efficiently and effectively in fast-paced environment.

In addition:

- ❑ Generated $50,000 in revenue savings for the company by completing eighteen, rather than fourteen, buildings by deadline.
- ❑ Reduced labor costs by 25% by hiring two Sheetrock companies and instigating competition.
- ❑ Accurately ordered and delivered materials, finding the best supplier prices, ensuring no materials were wasted, and achieving consistent cost savings.
- ❑ Delegated duties to various subcontractors, completed estimates, monitored materials and equipment on daily basis, and managed supply houses. Interfaced with owners and architects.

I will stop by the sales office on Friday, and if we cannot meet then, perhaps we can arrange a time in the near future.

Sincerely,

Melissa Sumner

TAMMY SHANAHAN

1 Melbourne Way, Denver, CO 33333 303.555.1111
ts@qway.net

March 17, 20__

Ms. Kathleen McCoy
Vice President, Kijo Corporation
1 Pikes Peak, CO Springs, CO 00000

Dear Ms. McCoy:

I have led the successful turnaround of three Fortune 100 companies and nine nationally recognized firms since 1990. You may not recognize my name, but my financial direction and leadership anchored the turnarounds at these organizations. I am eager to take on another challenge.

Your executive recruiting firm is recognized nationally for helping Fortune 500 corporations secure strong leaders and senior-level executives. Following more than a decade in a principal role with Anderson Consulting and McKinsey, I am looking for a company that would be interested in my leadership as a senior executive.

Two employers over the past 17 years
* Anderson Consulting   * McKinsey & Associates

Nine client companies (accompanied by outstanding references) that I have consulted for

Chrysler	Sprint Nextel	Hewlett-Packard
Dole	Cardinal Health	Allstate Insurance
Frito-Lay	Delphia	Nucor

My educational qualifications
MBA, Unversity of Michigan, 1988
BS in Finance, Northwestern University, 1986

Maximizing shareholder earnings/growth management/financial integrity
These are the three critical strengths I bring to the table. I am well connected with Wall Street and have been personally involved with positioning three companies in the past four years to go public (including drafting a 230-page financial summary and pro forma). Finally, I have spent 60% of my time over the last five years in the international arena, helping position companies to maximize foreign market potential.

****

Certainly I do not want to waste precious time for either of us. Should you come across a client seeking executive-level leadership that could take advantage of my qualifications and verifiable track record, feel free to contact me and I will forward a detailed, highly confidential resume with supporting documentation. I am seeking a position with a minimum compensation package of $200,000 and equity stock options based on performance.

Thank you for taking the time to review this letter. I look forward to hearing from you if you feel an opportunity might exist that would benefit one of your client companies.

Sincerely,

Tammy Shanahan

KIM TYNAN

1 Melbourne Way, Tulsa, OK 33333 303.555.1111
kt@mw.org

[sent via email]

Dear Mr. Grogel:

A few months ago, I completed the sale of EMC Inc., a company that, in four years of leadership, I successfully turned into a highly profitable and much desired operation. Although I have been offered a similar role with another subsidiary of EMC, I would like to explore career opportunities in building technology-based organizations. In anticipation of opportunities you may have for a senior operations or manufacturing executive, I enclose my resume for your consideration. Recent accomplishments include:

- Significant turnaround of EMC, resulting in a 1,250% increase in profitability and successful sale to the industry leader.

- Intense process and quality control reengineering effort, which led to PCS WIFI 300 certification and a 90% improvement in procedure compliance.

- Launch of a massive facility expansion and operational streamlining initiative, which boosted sales 63%.

As my achievements demonstrate, one of my greatest strengths lies in my ability to take a new or floundering operation and nurture it quickly into profitability. Throughout my career I have succes applied the principles of growth management, staff development, and business administration to real-life corporate issues. The cornerstones of my management philosophy are excellent communication, team spirit, training, and motivation.

Be advised that my recent compensation has averaged $330,000, but my requirements are flexible, depending upon location, job responsibilities, and other factors.

As a follow-up to this correspondence, I will call you next week to determine if my qualifications meet your needs at this time. As I have not yet discussed my plans with EMC, I would appreciate your discretion in this matter.

Sincerely,

Kim Tynan

Mark Young
111 Wylie Street, Danachestnut, TN 00000

June 1, 20__

Ms. Roberta Alexander
Director of Marketing, Leap Communications
101 Dallas Street, Suite 600
Nashville, TN 00000

Dear Roberta:

As competitive a market as wireless communications is, a strong sales leader is always in demand. A sales leader who understands the product offering, the needs of the customer, and how to connect the two is a differentiator in the sales arena. Also, one who can effect change and motivate and keep the sales associates on track is critical to meeting and exceeding sales objectives.

My track record of performance demonstrates consistent advancement in the sales field over the past fourteen years within the telecommunications industry. In each of my positions, I have surpassed every previous year's performance by a significant percentage. I accomplished this through opening new markets in competitive areas, successfully positioning product brands, and conducting qualitative market research allowing for effective strategic planning and program implementation. This methodology is a highly transferable skill. Of specific note may be the following indicators of the sales results I've produced for my employers:

- Implemented strategic selling practices that directly increased previous single-digit annual growth rate to consistent double-digit percentages annually for the past four years in highly competitive field.
- Successfully negotiated first-time multiyear contract with Fortune 50 banking institution representing 7% in annual revenues to company; secured ranking as #1 sales account executive corporatewide.
- Effectively turned around annual sales loss of 19% to growth in excess of 22% per year in two vertical market segments, through solution selling strategies.

I am certain these are the types of results I could quickly produce for your company as a senior sales manager. I look forward to the opportunity to discuss your hiring objectives and my qualifications in a personal interview and will contact you to arrange a convenient time. Thank you in advance for your consideration.

Sincerely,

Mark Young

Tiffany Randolph

111 Wylie Street, Danachestnut, TN 00000

February 20, 20___

Mr. Mike Torres
President, HCA
101 Main Street, Suite 600
Nashville, TN 00000

Dear Mike:

I understand you are seeking a sales manager to lead pharmaceutical sales within HCA's hospital network. As a medical/pharmaceutical account manager and area trainer managing a large territory in the Dallas area, I offer quantifiable accomplishments based on my experience with Merck, a Fortune 100 leader in health-care solutions.

Over the past two years, I produced $3.2 million in sales, attained back-to-back President Club awards, and was appointed to Merck's Field Advisory Council. One thing that has made me particularly successful is the strategic sales approach: researching the needs and objectives of the target market and matching our offerings to those needs.

Here are some specific accomplishments I have realized over the past few years:

Market Research: Evaluated potential markets for new product launches with powerful prelaunch analyses and competitive research. Assessed opportunities for line extensions and new product indications. Identified high-value physicians and provider segments with powerful and interactive market segmentation. Derived more insight from primary market research analysis on physician and patient panel data.

Sales Force Effectiveness: Combined distribution channel and sales force performance data to permit sales managers to adjust to shifts in market share positions and accurately and promptly deploy sales reps with better visibility into sales, physicians, and market information. Improved sales force effectiveness and call plan execution by targeting the highest-value physicians with focused detailing messages and promotions.

Managed Care Analysis: Identified the managed care users and plans that were most instrumental in the product's success and each territory's effectiveness. Interactively analyzed the plan reach and depth of coverage in a market in order to draw up improved contracts and to better target those plans offering the greatest potential for the products. Directed the sales force to the highest-value in-network physicians in order to maximize contract pull-through effectiveness.

Mike, facing challenging responsibilities with creativity based on strategy andsatisfying customer needs is my primary focus. I'd like to meet and discuss the ways in which I can contribute my experience and energy to HCA. I will give you a call next Wednesday, and I look forward to speaking with you.

Sincerely,

Tiffany Randolph

To: Matt Rounder

From: Chase Papier

Date: August 29, 20__

Subject: Spherion's NextGen Strategy

Financial leaders today need to be integral strategists in the profitable growth of interdependent corporate entities as they move into a more consolidated marketplace of fewer but larger industry leaders. If you have a need for a visionary senior-level executive with a cross-functional background in finance, sales, marketing, start-ups, joint-venture negotiations, and public/private financing, we should talk.

Currently I am the senior vice president of finance for a Fortune 100 company in the consumer products industry, and I have been instrumental in the origination of highly imaginative *and* highly profitable financial management programs achieved through motivational leadership blended with sound financing and creative thinking.

The following accomplishments reflect the absolute value that I can bring to Spherion's current and long-term objectives:

- Created a financial model instrumental in the development of a $112 million multidivision company from a money-losing group of lesser revenue-generating and profitable SBUs.

- Negotiated and closed an exclusive joint-venture agreement with a complementary Fortune 30 company to exploit a gap in the sales channel that was profitable in the second quarter of operation.

- Staffed major operating departments with their own controllers to provide analytical support to the department head while facilitating the flow of information to and from the centralized finance team.

- Implemented a companywide business planning process that included (1) corporate initiative prioritization, (2) operating and capital planning, and (3) performance and productivity reporting.

Should you seek a senior financial leader who will make an immediate and positive impact on operations, revenue streams, and profit margins, I would like to discuss the opportunity. I look forward to speaking with you soon.

Sincerely,

Chase Papier

TANYA SELHOST

1 Madison Way, Irvine, CA 91111 949.555.1111
cd@qway.net

January 17, 20__

Ms. Pam Goodwin
Senior Vice President, Cocoa Corporation
999 John Carpenter Freeway
Las Colinas, TX 72222

Dear Ms. Goodwin:

I understand you may be seeking a sales leader for the consumer division of Cocoa, and I would like to speak with you about my interest. I am a sales executive with a history of outstanding professional sales and management achievement. I offer a proven track record with over sixteen years' experience in the consumer products industry. As an influential leader who creates high-performing sales teams focused on excellent results, customer centricity. and shareholder value, I have achieved results that brought Diaar Corporation to new levels of profitability. I am regarded as an organizational leader who develops and cultivates valuable partnerships and creates strategic alliances.

For the past three years, I have served as vice president for sales and marketing of Diaar Corporation. I was recruited to plan and implement an aggressive sales and marketing program to grow domestic consumer sales; under my leadership, revenue has increased by over 55%, with a 320% growth rate for the health/beauty product lines.

Before joining Diaar, I served as the director of sales for P&G, a multi-million-dollar consumer products company with countless high-brand products. There I was accountable for marketing, sales, and partnering with key accounts; I led my team in reengineering the company's strategies; and we grew revenue more than 180% while fostering alliances with two new strategic partners.

I also served as the director of marketing with Kimberly-Clark, where I was accountable for all consumer marketing of the North America retail businesses (more than $600 million). My team identified and captured new business through aggressive marketing tactics and generated over 31% in incremental revenues. We were successful in differentiating the company from the competition by launching a unique advertising and packaging campaign targeted at the male 30–37 market segment.

I launched my career with the worldwide leader in publishing, Time Warner, and earned a series of fast-track promotions. Taking part in the company's key corporate vision, I contributed to the strategy accountable for expanding market share from 8% to 21%.

I also possess an executive MBA from Emory University.

I look forward to speaking with you and will contact you next Monday afternoon to discuss your needs in greater detail.

Best regards,

Tanya Selhost

Dawn B.B. McCarter

101 Bobby Way • Houston, TX 77777 • dbbm@htbfre.com

February 8, 20__

Paul Stanley
Stanley & Associates
1 Birmingham Street
Birmingham, MI 48207

Dear Mr. Stanley:

Today's leaders in product management need to understand both how to create profits in their business and how their products create profits. If you need a visionary manager who has proven to be able to accomplish both of these things, we should get together to discuss options.

The following accomplishments reflect what I am able to bring to your client, Goldrend Port:

I have seven years of experience in product management for a Fortune 75 consumer products company with high brand awareness, which was the winner of numerous consumer product awards. Below are specific areas of expertise and experience I have accumulated within this position:

- Segmentation targeting
- Financial forecasting
- Channel development
- Collateral, displays, and marcom
- Total communications strategist

- Offer development
- Advertising
- Sales promotion
- New product rollout
- Strategic planning

  o Synthesized health and beauty segment data from numerous sources, developing competitive profiles on key competitors. Extensively employed data from IRI, industry analyses and literature, and feedback from sales force and consumer focus groups, among others. Knowledge was employed to inform new product selection, guide market research, and refine product launch plans.
  o Evaluated key retail clients' product segment strengths and weaknesses; cooperated with key retail clients to develop strategies and guidelines to modify and complement in-process product lineup.
  o Negotiated and implemented private label/branded consumer product agreements, guidelines, and contracts with both retail clients and suppliers.
  o Developed and formally presented key channel strategies with major retail clients.

I will call you Thursday, and perhaps we can find a time in the next two weeks to meet and discuss the opportunity further.

Sincerely,

Dawn B.B. McCarter

Mark Ludwig

9011 Lakeview • New Orleans, LA 00000 • ml@glfhp.com

May 20, 20__

Grant Goodwin
Goodwin & Associates
3 Irving Road
Addison, TX 75240

Dear Mr. Goodwin:

Thank you so much for speaking with me regarding the director of IT position you are seeking to fill. During the past eleven years I have led the MIS operations for an Inc. 50 company. Based on what I saw in the description of the position and the information you shared, this looks like an opportunity that is worth exploring for both of us.

My experience in this industry has reached the ten-year milestone. Below are a few career highlights and accomplishments:

o Expert in the design, development, and delivery of cost-effective, high-performance technology solutions to meet challenging business demands for well-recognized international corporations including Motorola and Hewlett-Packard. Extensive qualifications in all facets of project life-cycle development, from initial feasibility analysis and conceptual design through documentation, implementation, and user training/enhancement.

o Equally effective organizational leadership, team building, and project management experience—introducing out-of-the-box thinking and problem-solving analysis to improve processes, systems, and methodologies currently in place to exceed business goals and to perpetually delight shareholders and customers.

o Conversion of existing MS Access–based applications to a web-centric environment using Oracle 8i, ASP, and Active X documents.

o Implementation of Cisco's Secure Virtual Private Network solution to replace long-distance data lines used to provide remote connectivity to the company's servers, and collaboration with the chief medical officer and epidemiologists to develop software used for medical record abstraction and data quality analysis.

On paper, this looks like a good mutual fit. Please expect my call later this week, and we can set up a time to discuss it further.

Sincerely,

Mark Ludwig

Lisa Councilman

3 Dallas Way
Grapevine, TX 75555
(972) 555-5555

September 3, 20__

Mr. Kevin Taylor
430 Houston Way
Houston, TX 78444

Dear Mr. Taylor:

Thank you for speaking with me this week. The new retail channel launch your joint venture is planning to execute is indeed groundbreaking and exciting. Below are some of my career highlights and qualifications for your reference:

AREAS of EXPERTISE:

- Multiunit manager for best-in-class retailer with premium brand awareness and reputation.
- Recruiting, training, and developing staff to high performance levels.
- Scheduling employees in accordance with customer traffic and demand.
- Displaying eye-catching merchandise and planograms to increase impulse purchasing and impact sales.
- Reducing costs and shrinkage to ensure optimum profitability.
- Overseeing all functions pertaining to operations including sales, adherence to company policy, controlling shrinkage, maintaining inventory levels, customer service, and strategic planning.

CAREER HIGHLIGHTS:

- Lowest turnover in region of 11 districts and 145 stores.
- P&L responsibility for 36 Borders stores in the southeast. With sales of $219 million, led field management team of district managers, area marketing managers, regional human resources manager, and recruiters.
  - Increased market share from 18% to 23% and controlled costs during industrywide sales downtrend.
  - Increased customer service scores through a focus on a selling culture and implementation of new customer service standards.
- Achieved 123% of revenue objectives.
- Instrumental in the success of 7 new store launches.
- Slashed budget expenditures by 11.7% while gaining enhanced productivity.
- Invited as key speaker at company's conference in recognition of outstanding performance.

If you believe these accomplishments fit into your plans, I'd certainly like to discuss the opportunity with you. Please contact me at your earliest opportunity.

Sincerely,

Lisa Councilman

Mike Gusola

101 Waco Way, Waco TX 75555 tr@erc.org

April 11, 20__

Mr. Jamie Smith
RTC Consumer Products, Inc.
1 Addison Drive
Addison, TX 75240

Dear Mr. Smith:

Russell Wentworth provided me with your name and thought it might be beneficial if we got together and discussed your recruiting effort in database management.

I have been the data warehouse manager for the past four years with Caber Consulting, and I possess an in-depth knowledge of the functional and data needs of e-businesses. Below are a few career highlights:

- Well-versed in Oracle (Oracle Express, Oracle Reporter, Oracle Financial), Oracle tools, and Erwin products. Data migration experience using Informatica, C++, Java, Corba, multidimensional database, JavaScript, Oracle Web server, and Java. Exceptional use of CASE tools as part of an overall development effort.

- Extensive knowledge of DBMS: Oracle RDBMS, SQL, PL/SQL, and STAR Schema Modeling. Experienced in UNIX operating system, Microsoft PC operating systems including NT, desktop productivity software, and client/server system architecture.

- Proven ability to assemble and mobilize project teams, building consensus among multidisciplinary technical and functional teams in the rapid development and implementation of data warehousing solutions. Recognized by managers and colleagues as a strong, positive leader and a sharp strategic thinker.

- Led focus group that created systems designed to eliminate an average of three hours of downtime. Monitored and modified systems, achieving weekly labor costs savings of $72,000.

- Developed and implemented an Electronic Data Input (EDI) ordering system for U.S. Navy within six weeks. Achieved $25 million annual order from Navy by meeting the established deadline.

Based on what Russell shared with me, this is an opportunity worth discussing for both of us. I will call you at the end of the week and see if we can set up some time to meet next week.

Thanks in advance for your consideration, Mr. Smith.

Mike Gusola

Rick Wernstein

14 Davison, Detroit, MI 48888 313.555.0000

August 29, 20___

Mr. Mason Marano
Marano and Associates, Ltd.
21 Peachtree Street
Atlanta, GA 33333

INSURANCE SALES PROFESSIONAL

**B.S.B.A./Financial Planning, Insurance, and Investment Sales/Increased Customer Base
Pioneered Efforts in New Territories/Multi-Million-Dollar Producer**

Dear Mr. Marano:

I led insurance sales at two Fortune 200 insurance providers and bring with me an extensive roster of clients. I am now seeking to work with a new insurance provider, and with the new market offers Marano and Associates is now launching, this is where I am interested in going.

While at both Farmer's and Allstate:

o   Landed 600+ new accounts throughout the Georgia and South Carolina region over a four-year period, representing more than $12 million in new business.

o   Millionaire Club 1994; 93 paid apps, $25,447 paid premium.

o   Monthly activity average = 65 total apps (30 auto, 15 fire, 10 life, 10 health).

o   Took initiative and developed promotional materials, grew territories by up to 45 percent, achieved a 100 percent client retention rate, and generated strong referral networks.

o   Capably positioned the companies represented as a preferred provider through extensive personal contact and a mutual respect for clients' time.

o   Generated $1.5 million in new business within a 22-month period. Prospected new customers via targeted direct mailings. Became involved in local events via memberships with various community organizations.

I look forward to discussing the opportunity in more detail in our next meeting. Thanks, Mr. Marano.

Rick Wernstein

David Grant

111 Thompson Street,
New York, NY 00000
dg@renrd.com

November 29, 20__

Ms. Bridgid Nesbit
Principal, CCF Ltd.
1 Baltimore Way
Baltimore, MD 00000

Dear Ms. Nesbit:

I understand you are undertaking a discreet recruiting effort for a chief operating officer for Taylor Industries. A mutual colleague of ours passed this information on, and if it is true, I might be interested in speaking with you about it. As the CEO and president of a Fortune 300 company with a track record of leadership and fast growth through strategic/tactical execution, I led teams that grew two companies from early stages to mid-cap size—two approaching $400 million per annum in top-line sales.

My career profile:

- Seven years' experience as CEO for Fortune 500 consumer products company.

- Twenty-three years in consumer products and packaging.

- Over fourteen years' related business management and marketing experience with a proven track record in building, supporting, and managing relationships across functional teams and corporate hierarchies.

- Experience in leading and managing successful organizations B2B and stewarding new marketing projects and proposals.

- Supervised, coordinated, oversaw, and represented complete marketing and advertising initiatives for publication and media for the community at large and monitored all press releases and printed material for distribution over a 200-mile radius.

- Entrepreneurial experience in managing and marketing new business development, including finance; start-up operations, and successful turnarounds.

My board is allowing me, discreetly, to explore an opportunity that fits my career objectives and gets me closer to the mid-Atlantic region. Let's talk soon and determine if indeed there is a fit.

Best regards,

David Grant

Franklin Horner
1111 Tampa Road • Oldsmar, FL 33556 • mb@yahaa.com • 813-555-1212

March 2, 20__

Nika Niksirat
Director of Recruiting
Limited Brands, Inc.
nn@wc.com

Dear Ms. Niksirat:

I am very interested in joining The Limited family of retail businesses. The Limited represents a best-in-class retail experience, and this is a team I want to support and help grow. I have worked in retail for some time and have developed excellent retail skills.

I have worked at The Gap and Sharper Image for my entire retail career. Some key accomplishments:

o *Number one salesman for four straight years.*

o *Promoted from sales associate to key sales associate.*

o *Independently opened and closed store, maintained sales records, and performed banking functions and evening deposits.*

o *Sales expertise in all areas of the store including cosmetics, women's, men's, children's, and junior's clothing; women's shoes;, housewares; jewelry; and accessories.*

o *Assisted store manager with store displays, merchandising, and sales promotions.*

o *Enhanced customer service and increased profits by suggestive selling and extensive knowledge of store products, primarily in women's shoes, women's clothing, and cosmetics.*

o *Consistently solved problems to customer satisfaction in this fast-paced sales environment.*

o *Professionally advised customers on the appropriate merchandise to meet their needs.*

o *Promoted repeat customers by establishing customer rapport and conducting follow-up as needed.*

o *Assisted in scheduling sales associates and determining goals for counter and sales associates. Assisted with initiating and executing special events. Responsible for achieving personal weekly and monthly goals through sales presentations, product knowledge, and promotional activities.*

Please expect my call later this week. In the meantime, I will shop some of your stores for ideas. Thanks!

Franklin Horner

David Watsky

Denver, CO
ldade@ert.com

May 2, 20__

HUMAN RESOURCES & TRAINING PROFESSIONAL

James Roller
VP Employee Relations
ING Inc.
14 Elm Street
Lakewood, CO 80000

Dear Mr. Roller:

I have followed the growth that ING has realized and now see that the employee count in this region is up over 200. As you recruit for a director of human resources, in both employee development and recruiting, please consider my accomplishments and how they potentially fit into your organization.

I have strong HR generalist experience with a proven talent in the development and implementation of training programs for exempt and nonexempt personnel, as well as a proven ability to develop material, impart knowledge, and update programs as needed.

- Strong research and analytical abilities; notable experience in the management and reduction of costs related to liability and insurance.
- Recruiting activities included all aspects of screening, interviewing, hiring, and orientation for union and nonunion staff.
- Continuously updated knowledge relevant to workers' compensation, ADA, EEO, Family Medical Leave Act, OSHA, DOT, etc.; developed and implemented new procedures to ensure compliance.
- Benefits administration experience includes program development, maintenance of costs through negotiations, and the development/implementation of alternative benefit programs.
- Assets in collective bargaining activities; successfully administered benefits to assist in successful negotiation.
- Generated ongoing bottom-line savings through the introduction of various cost-cutting programs.

In addition, my team facilitated seventeen focus groups targeting the executive team, nursing managers, new employees, and experienced employees. The purpose of the focus groups was to gather current state/gap analysis from a selected population who touched the talent acquisition, orientation, and assimilation process. We then developed a report that identified all the gaps by process, current cycle time, and best practices with desired cycle time. The goal of the workshop is to prioritize the gaps in the current process and develop a project plan for future work.

Recruiting: Through the optimization of technology and research, we were able to reduce the cycle time by 30 days and increase the candidates presented/to hire rate by 80%. We also provided a comprehensive report that provided the organization with technology solutions, process redesign recommendations, program design recommendations, recruiting metrics, and a project plan to help them optimize their talent acquisition process.

I will contact you at the end of the week and see if we can meet to discuss the opportunity further.

Sincerely,

David Watsky

Lee Andrews

3000 Shawnee Lane
Drayton Plains, MI 48888
(248) 555-5555

May 6, 20__

Mr. William Stanhouse
Cameo Rehabilitation
1900 Main Street
Clarkston, MI 48888

Dear Mr. Stanhouse:

Cameo Rehabilitation has built some wonderful facilities in the Detroit area, and the market here seems to be very receptive to the contribution you have made. I am very interested in joining the Cameo team. I completed my degree in physical therapy and am anxious to join the workforce full-time. I have completed several internships in the field, and some of my accomplishments are highlighted below:

- National Board for Certification in Occupational Therapy, No. 00668127.
- Michigan Board of Occupational Therapy, License No. 0231794.
- Performed analysis for all clients in the industrial rehab program.
- Identified the physical, environmental, psychophysical, and psychosocial risk factors for clients employed in industrial and office settings.
- Recommended controls for process flow, safety equipment, and ergonomically designed workstations/seating used to reduce risk hazards in industrial and office settings.
- Able to perform Swedish, deep tissue, sports, and medical massage, as well as reflexology and table shiatsu.
- Responsible for work conditioning, job simulation, job coaching, and job performed VDT ergonomic analysis and facilitated training sessions on injury prevention, posture, body mechanics, joint protection, and energy conservation techniques to improve work efficiency/productivity and injury reduction.
- Educated clients on the abnormal illness behavior cycle and its correlation to pain management Collaborated with engineering, safety, and management to integrate workplace operations, processes, and conditions to reduce the number of low back strain and musculoskeletal injuries with nursing staff and material handlers.
- Independently provided services in the community. Set independent schedule, including productivity that was consistently 10 to 15% above productivity requirement.

My resume is attached, but these highlights will give you a quick snapshot of my career thus far. Please contact me at your earliest opportunity, or I will call you next week to touch base.

Sincerely,

Lee Andrews

LEIGH ANN EPPERSON
1 Madison Way, Irvine, CA 91111 949.555.1111
lae@rrr.com

Mr. Claye Colton
Senior Director, IT Systems
999 John Carpenter Freeway
Las Colinas, TX 72222

Dear Mr. Colton:

I have researched your corporation and am impressed with your company"s management style and reputation in the employment industry. I am very interested in exploring job opportunities with your organization, as I believe I could make a significant contribution in a company like yours.

Please allow me to briefly tell you about myself. I have ten years of experience as a civil engineer. My diverse experience in engineering, operations, and project management makes me a fairly close-fit candidate to what your seeking. My specific expertise is focused on public utilities, and I am a registered Professional Engineer #GPE000X, State of Texas. My specific skills are in:

- Problem solving
- Budget administration
- Computer systems
- Supervision and training
- Engineering and project management
- Operations and financial management
- Organizational administration
- Quality and productivity improvement

A copy of my resume is enclosed. I would be happy to meet with you and discuss my qualifications in more detail. I will call you in a few days to see if an interview might be possible. In the meantime, thank you for your time and consideration.

Please consider my qualifications, as summarized here and on the attached resume, for a position of engineer with your firm. I believe that the experience I have gained over the past six years operating my own engineering consulting firm and the training and knowledge I received as an electrical engineering major in college can be of enormous benefit to your organization.

In addition, I have enjoyed a reputation for being a very hard-working, intelligent, and industrious individual. My motivation is to utilize my accumulated experience and knowledge to the fullest extent possible, becoming a valuable asset for the right company. I would appreciate the opportunity to interview with you. Thank you for your consideration.

Sincerely,

Leigh Ann Epperson

Gaylord Perrington
3 Dragon Way, West Palm Beach, FL 33409

Clinical Director: MANAGED CARE • PROVIDER NETWORKS • SYSTEM INTEGRATIONS • QUALITY IMPROVEMENT • COMMUNITY-BASED NETWORKS • COMMUNITY RELATIONS

December 14, 20___

Parker Jayson
Trinity Support Center
Lewisville, TX 75555

Dear Mr. Jayson:

Health-care patients deserve great care from health-care providers, and the health-care providers must keep that responsibility in the forefront while managing the business as well. Based on my performance record, I am a very viable candidate for your health-care administrator position at Trinity.

Reviewing my credentials, you will notice I have several years' experience at Presbyterian Hospital in Plano. While I am happy there and the business is going well, I am actually seeking a new challenge. Below are some accomplishments that might align with your needs:

- Increased revenues by 120% through proactive marketing campaigns and the establishment of three new revenue sources including physical rehabilitation, occupational and speech therapy department, mental health counseling, and substance abuse counseling centers.
- Decreased housekeeping costs by 23% while increasing overall staff productivity by 29%.
- Developed a multistate health-care system, consisting of 1,024 beds, with gross revenue exceeding $161 million.
- Acted as resource in development of $9.5 million bond issue.
- Had regional P&L responsibility, directing a multi-million-dollar operation consisting of 40 outpatient rehabilitation facilities. Recruited 7/98 with key responsibilities to include revenue generation; new business development on a national scale; personnel recruitment, training, and supervision; and development/execution of strategic operations and marketing plans.

I am seeking to experience a new challenge and replicate my past success at Presbyterian Hospital. My references are very strong in many disciplines, and my standing at Presby Plano is excellent. Should you feel there is a potential fit, please call me at your earliest opportunity.

Sincerely,

Gaylord Perrington

7

Responses to Job Postings and Classified Ads

It's amazing how much has changed in the way information is exchanged over the past 12 years. My first career reference guide barely mentioned online job postings, and that was only in 1997. A decade later, information exchanged is so rapid and access to data is so much more widespread—not just for you and me, but for everyone, which is both good and bad in a job search.

While networking is still a very primary source of moving on to a new opportunity, it has more to do with sponsorship than with the quantity of leads. No other source will expose you to as many opportunities as the postings online. Couple that with the many applicants who lack the attention to detail needed to craft a to-the-point cover letter and resume, and this medium will open many more doors than were previously available.

Responses to online postings present their own challenges, many of which are highlighted in Chapter 3. Long-winded, "me-oriented" letters are likely to get lost in that black hole. And formatting with different-size fonts, bullet points, and italicized/bold typeface won't make the translation from MS Word to the online posting service format.

Create a special resume in plain text with no special fonts or bullets (use dashes for bullets, for example).

Coury Mascagni
5903 13th Street NE, #1617   Home: (222) 555–0234
Louisville, KY 55232

MANAGEMENT PROFILE

Distinguished management career developing business systems, processes, and organizational infrastructures that have improved productivity, increased efficiency, enhanced quality, and strengthened financial results. Expertise in identifying and capitalizing on opportunities to enhance corporate image, expand market penetration, and build strong operations. Broad-based general management, financial management, and project management qualifications. Outstanding record in personnel training, development, and leadership.

— Strategic Planning and Tactical Execution
— Productivity and Efficiency Improvement
— Business and Performance Reengineering
— Leadership Development and Career Pathing
— Corporate Culture and Organizational Development
— Consensus Building and Cross-Functional Relations
— Service Design and Delivery Systems
— Customer-Driven Management

PROFESSIONAL EXPERIENCE

NORTHWEST AIRLINES, St. Paul, Minnesota   1997 to Present

Fast-track promotion throughout 20+ year tenure, ascending from field to corporate operations in both start-up and large-scale business locations. Built successful business partnerships, managed cross-functional communications, and designed/implemented proactive organizational development, employee performance, and corporate culture programs. Key projects and achievements have included:

Start-up and High-Growth Operations Management

— Held full decision-making responsibility for the daily operations of the St. Paul facility, Northwest's largest center. Led the operation through a period of significant growth, market expansion, and diversification including several mergers, divestitures, and volume increases.
— Introduced cost management, conflict resolution, and corporate culture change initiatives for the start-up Yellowstone operation (1,000 personnel and 65 flights daily). Resolved long-standing communication issues, streamlined systems, and created a highly successful and profitable operation.
— Planned construction of 15,500-space parking facility for the St. Paul operation. Worked with city officials, designers, contractors, company personnel, and service providers throughout project cycle.

Business Process Reengineering

— Orchestrated a complete reengineering of the Ramp Tower operation, supporting seven major facilities nationwide. Designed/implemented programs to streamline processes, increase performance and decision-making authority, and position the operation as a cooperative business partner with core operations. Program is currently being implemented throughout Northwest's U.S. operations.
— Spearheaded complete automation of all administrative functions for 6,500-employee St. Paul operation. Significantly improved the timeliness and accuracy of key operating, customer, and financial information.

Employee Development, Communications, and Liaison Affairs

Career Progression

Northwest Express Yellowstone Manager (1997 to Present)
St. Paul Ramp Tower Manager (1996 to 1997)
Duty Manager (1995 to 1996)
Station Analyst (1995)
Supervisor/Ramp Tower Coordinator (1988 to 1995)
Lead Customer Services Agent (1984 to 1988)
Senior Customer Services Agent (1979 to 1984)
Revenue Accounting Clerk (1978 to 1979)
Flight Attendant (1977 to 1978)

EDUCATION

UNIVERSITY OF MINNESOTA
Candidate for Doctoral Degree in Community Psychology, 1995 to Present

Emphasis in Organizational, Sociological, and Psychodynamic Theory/Application

Bachelor of Science in Psychology and Sociology, 1995
Magna Cum Laude Graduate; Phi Kappa Phi Honor Society; Golden Key National Honor Society
Outstanding Scholarship Award; State College Scholastic Achievement Award

Many job-hunting sites, including Careerbuilder.com and Monster.com, offer subscriptions to job alerts based on the criteria you set up. Take advantage of this feature! This is a wonderful tool for passively receiving leads that are good fits for your skills. To enjoy these features, you have to subscribe as a member and fill out the criteria for your job search. The job site will then perform searches according to your specified criteria.

Many independent Web pages are dedicated to job hunting online. You can set up your own Web page, directing prospective employers to that page, or look at your targeted employer's page; they frequently have job postings listed. However, the best methods of contact are still personal, because frequently the best and higher-level positions are not posted. However, they are inexpensive to access, and you may identify a lead through e-mail contact with hiring managers or other job seekers.

On the Web, conduct several different searches for both job search keywords and the industry or discipline in which you specialize. Also, contact the local newspaper for additional online sources specific to your metropolitan area.

The top sites that feature these opportunities include the following:

- Monster.com (www.monster.com)
- CareerBuilder (www.careerbuilder.com)
- Jobs.com (www.jobs.com)
- America's Job Bank (www.jobsearch.org)
- HotJobs (www.hotjobs.com)

Many employers discard any resume submitted without a letter. That's because a well-crafted cover letter communicates the message that the job is important to you. You will never be penalized for including a letter. When crafting your cover letter, pay careful attention to the employer's needs—the more customized the message in your letter, the greater the odds of receiving a favorable response.

When crafting your cover letter, here are some additional suggestions:

1. Write your letter in MS Word and then copy and paste it into the online window field. MS Word will automatically spell- and grammar-check your draft.

2. The letter should introduce you and your resume; don't repeat your resume content.

3. Keep the letter short.

4. Use language in your cover letter to exhibit your professional personality.

5. Follow up on particularly good fits by calling and asking to speak to someone about the position. Professional persistence pays off. It takes only a little research to find out who the contact is in a blind ad if you conduct some Internet research on the company or position.

6. Respond to ads if you have 50 percent or more of the skills described. The job description usually represents a company's wish list, but there's no guarantee they'll find anyone with 100 percent of the listed qualifications.

You may gain insight by looking at ads that don't necessarily match your background. You may see an ad that says, "Due to our expansion in the Northeast we are looking for . . ." You have just learned of an expanding company that might need you. Review papers that have good display ads such as the *Los Angeles Times*, the *Chicago Tribune*, and other major Sunday editions. Tactically, this is an interesting suggestion. Follow the thought process above and call them.

Many classified ads list a fax number but no company name or main number. They encourage you to fax your resume but not to call them. In most companies a fax number is a derivative extension of the main number. If the fax number is 555–5479, there is a good chance that the main number is 555–5000 or 555–5400. With that, you can call them and hunt for information, write them a more interesting and industry-specific letter, and position yourself ahead of the people who didn't use this method.

Then, when you write them, write about the company, rather than just saying "I am answering your ad." If you mail a hard copy, package the resume and cover letter in a U.S. Priority Mail envelope so that it stands out, and you will be guaranteed to at least be reviewed, which is your first objective when answering an ad.

Though there are many great resources to help you in your online search, here are a few tips to keep in mind:

1. Have a good idea of what types of jobs you are seeking. That will make the search on these online sites narrower in scope and more productive. Have geography and keywords prepared in advance.

2. Have two resumes ready: a finished Microsoft Word document to send as an attachment and a nonformatted text-only resume to copy and paste in e-mail. The content should be the same, but the latter should be stripped of formatting that will not be preserved through the e-mail exchange.

3. Plan to post your resume at these sites as well as sending it directly to recruiters and employers.

4. Take the time to read and understand how the sites work before jumping in.

5. Print out copies of everything you see that is of interest. It will help you for future reference. Also, catalog the names of people to whom you send e-mails and resumes so that you don't send redundant applications.

6. Provide a personal e-mail address, not that of your current employer. Check your e-mail daily, as e-mail is commonly used for a first reply.

7. We will cover this in more detail later, but make sure the phraseology you use in your description of your experience and what you want to do is very concise. The folks reading these cover letters and resumes are doing so online and will not spend a lot of time on each one, so make it possible for them to get to your qualifications and objectives quickly and effortlessly.

David Taylor

1 Quarry Way   Stoneham, MA 00000 (508) 555-1111

July 16, 20__

Ms. Stephanie Smith
Senior Partner
Robert Half and Associates
1 Harbor Town
Boston, MA 00000

Dear Ms. Smith:

I am responding to your advertisement for a software applications specialist. Below is how I align with the requirements listed on your posting:

Position Requirements	Personal Accomplishments
Tests, evaluates, and finalizes specific software features and functions, with a primary emphasis on ensuring that software meets functional requirements.	At CMG, worked closely with developers and spent 1.5 years in software troubleshooting prior to most recent release.
Determines best means to deploy and support products, on a project basis, as they move from the testing/evaluation phase to the deployment phase.	With the MR.3 release, forecasted where support was most likely to be needed and worked with care to develop support and training program.
Works with a design team to test and analyze specific hardware or software combinations under consideration for use.	Took MR.3 release to three beta customer users and tested compatibility with most common server and application interchangeability.
Provides technical support in the evaluation of new clinical software products including performance testing, reliability testing, deployment requirements, cost analysis, manpower requirements, and maintainability.	Led the completion of manual of guidelines, budgeted for it, and completed interoperability testing and support cost estimates. One year later, we came in under budget in cost and care issues.
Provides support to staff/ and vendors involved in the deployment, installation, or repair of network hardware or software as projects move from design and planning to operational status.	Led team of four to support the deployment of latest software release, which resulted in over 80% satisfaction rate, above industry average for beta test.

My objective is to establish a time when we can meet together to discuss how I can add value to your operation. I realize how full your schedule must be, so I will take it upon myself to be in contact with your office within the next few days to discuss the possibility of an interview. Thank you for your consideration. I look forward to speaking with you soon.

Sincerely,

David Taylor

Patricia Arbor

I Castle Way, Fort Worth, TX 77777 817.555.1111

Response for LPN posting on Careerbuilder.com:

> ❑ Degree from an accredited school of nursing
>
> ❑ License to practice nursing in the state for which you are applying
> ❑ Current CPR. ACLS certification required within 90 days of employment
> ❑ Must demonstrate competency in current principles and practices clinically specific to critical care or medical surgical and rehabilitative and gerontological nursing

March 1, 20___

Dear Human Resources Manager:

I am very interested in joining your health-care team at Presbyterian Plano Hospital. My two employers since I completed my formal education are Highland Park General Hospital and Trinity Medical Center. In both positions as LPN, I have been recognized for five major achievements over the past decade:

1. Perfect attendance record—no absences or missed shifts.
2. Great reputation with all staff as team player willing to do what it takes, supported by references I am able to provide.
3. Very competent LPN medical skills—committed to continuous improvement.
4. Continued development in advanced learning skills and certifications.
5. Some PA training and a rotation in hospice care.

I will call you next Wednesday to introduce myself and discuss the opportunity in more detail. Thanks so much for your consideration. I believe I am a very strong candidate and sincerely think this opportunity is worth exploring for both of us.

Sincerely,

Patricia Arbor

Jaime Cantu
2 Lola Lane, Dallas, TX 75240 972.555.1111

Job Description

RRR Resources is now interviewing for Journey-level service Plumbers. Temp to Hire for a growing service company in the Dallas area. Full benefits included (medical, dental, and vision insurance, paid vacation, 401K enrollment, and referral bonuses). We can put you to work immediately! Send us your resume today!

Jaime Cantu is one of the most dependable, skilled plumbers I have ever employed. He has worked on over 500 new homes and has done a very reliable job for us.

Paul Parish, Director, Western Homes, TX

April 29, 20__

Dear Personnel Manager:

I am very interested in joining your team. I have worked for Western Homes for the past four years and am now returning to Houston for personal reasons. My work ethic, reputation, and quality of work have been at the very top within the industry in Dallas, and I would be happy to provide references to support this.

I was the lead plumber for the Frisco Trails development, a development of 2,000 homes that range from 2,500 to 4,500 square feet.

Please consider my qualifications and feel free to follow up with Mr. Parish at Western Homes. I will call you Monday to discuss the opportunity in more detail, and perhaps we can set up a meeting soon. I will be available anytime after May 10. I am looking forward to speaking with you soon.

Sincerely,

Jamie Cantu

Mark Quinn
3 Dragon Way, West Palm Beach, FL 33409

January 12, 20__

Pam Goodwin
Trinity Support Center
Boynton Beach, FL 33333

Dear Ms. Goodwin:

Your advertisement for a director of community support is of great interest to me and, based on your requirements, is a close fit to my experience.

I have spent the bulk of my career in the nonprofit sector and find that industry very rewarding. Most of that time I worked in the health-care area, raising funds for cancer research and for the Florida Heart Association. Here are some highlights keyed to your requirements:

College graduate preferred.	Graduated from FAU with degree in marketing.
Three to five years as a director or coordinator of volunteer services in an acute care, hospice, or nonprofit/foundation setting.	Served for four years as director for the South Florida branch of the Florida Heart Association, increasing fund-raising by over 46% over previous two-year period.
Excellent written and communication skills.	Led draft forums and petitions for new fund development; worked with state agency on co-op programs.
Schedule sponsor volunteers according to the Build Schedule created by development department.	Expanded largest volunteer network within state for nonprofit fund-raising.

I feel I have a very good, albeit peripheral, understanding of Trinity Medical and what your objectives are for this position. Based on my experience and accomplishments, this really is a terrific fit for Trinity and me.

Please give my background and potential some thought, and I will call you early next week to set up a meeting for us. Have a great week, Ms. Goodwin.

Sincerely,

Mark Quinn

GREG STARR   Beach Road One, Miami, Florida 33333 ▪ (954) 555-0000

March 19, 20__

Ms. Becky Hiebert
1 KC Way
1 Castle Hill Drive
Castle Hills, TX 75556

Dear Ms. Hiebert:

I am writing in response to your recent posting for Level 3 Security Engineer. Please accept this letter and accompanying resume as evidence of my interest in applying for this position with your company.

My enclosed resume clearly shows I have qualifying skills and abilities compatible with this position. Briefly, they are as follows:

❑ Implemented application-level security solutions on Solaris and Linux platforms.
❑ Implemented network-level and application-level security solutions using Cisco, Juniper, and Aventail security appliance platforms.
❑ Participated in and advised on security policy design with American Express.
❑ Performed systems, network, and application troubleshooting in support of global operations team.
❑ Developed and integrated systems management and monitoring tooling for the security infrastructure and use by the global operations team.

Nontechnically speaking, I also accomplished the following:

❑ Gathered requirements from top seven clients to develop custom applications.
❑ Coordinated and led the response to technology problems.

After you have the opportunity to review my resume I would like to meet with you to discuss how effectively I can contribute. Should you have any questions before scheduling an appointment, I may be reached at the number listed above.

Thank you very much for taking the time to review my resume and for your kind consideration. I look forward to speaking with you in the near future.

Sincerely,

Greg Starr

KIM TYNAN

1 Melbourne Way, Tulsa, OK 33333
303.555.1111
kt@mw.org

[sent via email]

Re: Champs Restaurant Manager for Oklahoma City, OK

Dear Champs Recruiting Group:

Currently I am managing an On The Border restaurant in the Tulsa area and am going to be relocating to Oklahoma City at the end of the month. I saw the posting for a manager for one of your new restaurants and am very interested in taking my experience from the Chili's family to a new organization.

Below are some highlights of my experience that closely match the objectives you're seeking:

- ❑ Responsible for smooth operation of the restaurant and lounge areas and equipment.
- ❑ Ensure customer satisfaction including dealing with complaints, special reservations, and meeting planning. We are ranked in the top 15% nationally in this area.
- ❑ Manage restaurant and lounge areas and equipment.
- ❑ Manage restaurant and lounge staff, delegating responsibilities, scheduling, disciplining, evaluating, hiring, training, and mentoring for future promotion possibilities. We have had the lowest turnover in the state of any restaurants in our corporate family.
- ❑ Execute budgetary responsibilities including forecasts, target worker-hours, labor forecasting, profit and loss accountability, cost control, inventories, and just-in time purchasing.

I have been very successful and feel this is a very good fit. I hope to hear from you soon.

Sincerely,

Kim Tynan

Debbie Caskey
dcaskey@www.com
922 555 0000

Recruiting Manager
Sprint Communications Company
Dallas, TX

Dear Recruiting Manager:

Attached is my resume, but here is a quick summary of how I line up with each of your objectives:

Your Requirements	My Accomplishments
Five to eight years' successful program/product management experience in the medical device industry. Proven track record of working with internal cross-functional teams resulting in successful outcomes/business growth with the customer base.	Worked for Fortune 100 company for six years in marketing and program management for new initiatives. Worked on multiple and future high-volume products with several disciplines, including marketing, engineering, sales, and finance.
Experience in the acute and extended care environments.	Worked for four years with HCA and am very familiar with the care environments.
Demonstrated experience selling and/or marketing programs in to the IDN environment. Ability to deal with physicians, nurses, and hospital administration with a variety of product segments.	Worked closely with the sales organization within HCA and am very comfortable working with physicians and all disciplines in health-care industry.
Minimum two years' supervisory experience building a team a plus.	Worked in management capacity for three years and in that time hired eight midlevel marketing managers; all are still with us and two were promoted.
Bachelor's degree required. Master's a plus.	MBA from TCU in business administration.

I have been responsible for developing and implementing strategies necessary to grow business within the integrated delivery network segment. As well, I interface with marketing teams and IDN sales directors to initiate programs for growth of multiple company business segments.

This appears to be a mutually great fit. I can also provide impeccable industry references. Bridging the gap between multiple disciplines and working to break ground on new initiatives are my passions. I am looking forward to speaking with you soon.

Sincerely,

Debbie Caskey

Chris Zach
1 Carrollton Way, Carrollton, TX 75243   chrisz@retter.com   214 555 0000

March 12, 20__

Adrian Ward
Merk Chemical
aw@ca.net

Dear Mr. Ward:

I am very interested in speaking with you about your recruiting effort to add a pharmaceutical sales associate for the north Texas area. Based on the objectives listed for this position, it is a very close fit to my experiences. I have attached my resume, but below are some highlights of my industry experience:

❑ Developed relationships with the physician/provider community in order to secure their referrals when a patient required a hearing test/hearing aids.

❑ Created a medical business model for the territory that resulted in over 14% year-over-year growth for three straight years. Exceeded sales results each year in territory.

❑ Created programs that ensured ENT physicians referred their patients to our clinics and used our medication first.

❑ Developed a team approach to accomplish increased physician referrals by persuading clinic audiologists to take ownership and assume responsibility for marketing outside their four walls.

❑ Created multiple sales and marketing programs and materials to support efforts with the physician''s clinics during each sales call, in lunch-and-learn presentations, and with each note written to a provider.

In addition to all of the above, I have a great deal of energy and a personal commitment to providing the highest level of service. I really enjoy the business, and one trademark of my success has been logging in more customer and hospital visits than my peers. I love venturing out in the field and recognize that as the key to success. I am looking forward to hearing back soon.

Sincerely,

Chris Zach

Elsie Coxon
mfrom@www.com
972 555 0000

Mark Johnson
Syly Learning Center

[sent via email]

Dear Mr. Johnson:

Although I graduated from high school with a 3.6 GPA, I had not always been so successful. During my freshman year, I struggled and had to have special tutoring to remedy early learning deficiencies from my elementary school days. I experienced firsthand the impact extra academic work can have and the extended value it provides for getting into college and ultimately contributing to success as an adult.

As a teacher, I enjoy the challenge of making learning an exciting and enjoyable process. My approach is to never forget the student perspective and to develop the empathy to relate to students to help them realize the importance of learning.

Some relevant highlights of my career include the following:

- Designed curriculum for designated caseload of students.
- Built rapport with student families.
- Designed prescription and reviews.
- Consistently provided conferences with parents and families.
- Floor-managed and coached staff.
- Instructed/tested as scheduled.
- Maintained daily schedule and recorded tasks in common repository.

I am very interested in taking on more work to help students achieve their ultimate goals. I can provide many references from students and their parents.

Sincerely,

Elsie Coxon

Sandy Smith
jmar@usafinance.net
954 555 0000

Re: Customer Service Representative Job Posting

I am writing to formally apply for the CSR position for which you are recruiting at USA Finance.

My past successes demonstrate strengths in working in a call center environment, being focused on the task at hand/expediency, solving customer problems, and assuming team leadership roles within the center.

I attended the following classes in the effort to hone my coaching and interpersonal management skills:

- Managing Conflict—AT&T School of Business, Course MS6431, completed July 2004.
- Managing People and Performance—AT&T School of Business, Course MD7601, completed October 1993.
- Certifications: Numerous technical and managerial courses: Managing Conflict, Managing People and Performance, Communications Workshop, Leadership for the Future, Achieving Communication Effectiveness, and Labor Relations (AT&T School of Business & Technology).

I have never been a maintainer, but rather I enjoy taking on a challenge, resolving problems, and being a part of the growth of a business. If you are seeking someone with a track record of putting out fires and improving service levels, I'd like to explore the possibility of joining your company. Thank you.

Sincerely,

Sandy Smith

Paul Helter

1 Brady Drive, Boston, MA 00000
(508) 555-5555

June 18, 20__

Valerie Sprinter
Director of Human Resources, CUSA
909 Dallas Parkway
Dallas, TX 75240

Dear Ms. Sprinter:

Experienced Team Leader with a Passion for Customer Service

I have been a team leader with ABC's call center for the past two years. One of the most important and difficult lessons I've learned during this time is how to create a high-energy, high-morale working environment. This area is not only where I excel, but it is truly my passion. As a manager, I love to get results—whether it's in building the team, training and developing the team members, or driving them to exceed performance goals.

I've had the pleasure of speaking with a few of the employees at CUSA. People really seem to like working there, because of the culture the company promotes. This not only impressed me, but also gave me extra incentive to apply for this position. I will call you next Wednesday to discuss the opportunity in more detail.

Sincerely,

Paul Helter

8

Writing to an Executive Recruiter

Without some knowledge of the recruiting industry, choosing an appropriate recruiter can be as difficult as choosing an employee. There are over 6,000 recruiters of some kind in the United States. Some are large chains such as Robert Half Inc., and some are private recruiters that are more like consultants. Here is a brief overview of the recruiting industry as it relates to doing a job search and developing your resume.

TYPES OF RECRUITING AGENCIES

Executive recruiters fall into two major categories: retained search firms and contingency employment agencies. Retained search firms specialize in senior-level professionals and executives. Traditionally, contingency agencies focus on the lower end of the hiring segment, from entry level through middle management. The two types are likewise different in the way they recruit and charge for their services.

Retained Search Firms

Retained search firms are hired by a company for a period of time. They are paid as consultants whether or not they fill the position the search is being conducted for. The employers, as with a contingency, pay these firms, but the retained firms act more like employees of the company, as many consultants do. They are less receptive to a candidate approaching them than is a contingency recruiter. Still, this is a channel worth pursuing.

One reason they are retained and paid is that they are searching for candidates for hard-to-fill positions, which takes time and money. There is no guarantee they will find them, and so they need some working capital to carry them through. A retained recruiter may get about a third of the employee's first-year salary. The salary range of a position a recruiter fills might vary from $150,000 to a senior-level executive earning millions.

Contingency Recruiting Agencies

Contingency agencies, such as Management Recruiters, charge a fee to the employer only when the candidate is hired. The contingency recruiter will generally perform some prescreening for the employer and then send a pool of candidates to the employer to screen and interview. Rates usually range from 20 to 30 percent of the employee's first-year salary. The salary level of a position a contingency firm fills can range from $40,000 to $150,000.

Here are some tips to be mindful of when working with executive recruiters:

- Don't ever sign an exclusive agreement with a recruiter.
- Don't pay a recruiter; that should come from the employer.
- Open up your geographical boundaries when reaching out to a recruiter. Rarely do recruiters live where the positions are for which they recruit. In fact, as a random example, a friend of mine is a recruiter in San Diego and he is currently searching for positions in Dallas, Charlotte, and Lawrence, Kansas.
- To identify recruiters, conduct some Internet searches and/or find a directory. Then, be proactive and manage the process. The candidate should be the one leading the search effort. To do this, you need to keep track of where your letters and resume have been sent, whom you have talked to, and what employers have been presented to you. Don't give permission to circulate your profile or send it out without your specific approval.
- Your cover letter is your window to appear professional and exhibit some personality. When recruiters believe that you are a real professional, they are more likely to think of you when an appropriate position opens. Cover letters provide both the personal and the professional touch. The letters also have the most impact if you address them to a person, rather than to a blind "To Whom It May Concern" address.
- When you do speak with a recruiter, approach the task as if you were actually interviewing with a hiring manager. If you are fortunate enough to gain the confidence of the recruiter, he or she may serve as a confidante; the more the recruiter knows about you, the easier it will be for him or her to describe you with passion and enthusiasm. Recruiters can also make effective advisors and mentors. With their knowledge of the industry, their fingers on the pulse of industry changes, and their contacts, you may also learn much about the industry. Be charming.
- Be fair to the recruiter. If you are not interested in a position or a reasonable fit for a position, be forthright so you do not waste anyone's time. This will still leave the door open for future opportunities. Be courteous and return all calls and e-mails in a timely way. Calls should be returned within 24 hours and e-mail within the same time frame, up to 48 hours.

- Be a source for recruiters to network to find great candidates. In my day job, I have been a source for two positions filled in different parts of the country for a California recruiter, though I have not worked directly with the firm. It's good business, facilitates networking for others, and, in the spirit of paying good deeds forward, will yield good things in the future for you.

David Ryan
101 Madison Avenue, NY, NY 10001
dryan@rewq.net

Ms. Renee Powers
RP Associates
1 Norfolk Way
Richmond, VA 20111

Dear Ms. Powers:

Marty Plank mentioned to me that you specialize in the health-care industry and that you might know of health-care companies looking for a regional operations manager. If so, please review my resume and consider introducing my credentials to them.

As an experienced and successful regional manager with HCA, I have a record of working efficiently with insurance partners, pharmaceuticals, and the medical staff within our group of hospitals.

My background includes:

- Seven years with HCA, having been promoted internally three times.
- Operational improvements in cost of labor and insurance claims, and an increase in customer/patient satisfaction.
- Top-line sales growth of over 20% annually for the past three years in our region.
- Hiring two hospital administrators, both of whom are still with us and who have improved performance over 35% each in their respective hospitals, with no turnover.

I have accomplished what I was hired to do here, and I am simply interested in exploring new challenges in the industry, in Virginia or even in Florida or Texas.

I'll give you a call next Wednesday to discuss this in more detail.

Sincerely,

David Ryan

Michelle Bristow

101 Eagles Way, Odessa, FL 33556

March 14, 20__

Ms. Maria Lane
Robert Haver Associates
14 Orlando Way
Orlando, FL 33409

Dear Ms. Lane:

Mike Jackson and some other colleagues of mine at Nokia have mentioned work you have done in this industry and in the state of Florida. We should talk soon.

My launch experience with the direct and indirect sales channels has been distinguished as the highest performing within the industry here:

• With management responsibility for the indirect channel, we boasted year-over-year growth of over 30% in the aggregate last year through new training and incentive programs with name-brand retailers like Best Buy, RadioShack, Circuit City, and Sound Advice.

• In the direct channel, we boasted higher productivity per store than any other state. We achieved this through improved hiring and disciplined but motivating performance management. This earned me the Regional Director of the Year award in 2007.

As you know, this is a turbulent industry, and I am simply trying to become aware of other opportunities that are out there—opportunities with first-tier carriers or retailers that would appreciate and benefit from my accomplishments.

I will call you next Thursday to discuss this in more detail, and, of course, feel free to contact me anytime.

Sincerely,

Michelle Bristow

David Heintzelman

1 Southlake Way
Southlake, TX 75555
(214) 555-5555

May 19, 20__

Mr. Randy McCutchan
Radar and Associates
1011 Dallas Parkway, Suite 1
Addison, TX 75240

Dear Mr. McCutchan:

The difference between average and superior performance in any organization always comes back to the quality of the people hired. Under my leadership as the director of human resources for P&R, we have realized results well above industry averages in employee retention, productivity per employee, and morale level. Some programs we drove to accomplish this include:

- Creating a teaching organization within our leadership group. While it cost more in time and resources on the front end, it resulted in more motivated and skilled employees. It's been the cornerstone of our success.
- Initiating special leadership, development, and other training programs to leverage personnel strengths and maximize people in each discipline.
- Changing the way we recruit based on behavioral interviewing, resulting in streamlined hiring practices, reduced cost per hire, and increased employee retention.
- Leading creative recruitment campaigns to identify best-qualified candidates from executive level to support staff, usually within highly competitive markets.
- Facilitating the integration of people from separate business units, creating a unified operation despite varying management styles and organizational structures.

The scope of my experience spans the entire HR function, including employee relations, staffing, retirement, benefits, succession planning, and performance management. Most significant is the way we integrated employee relations and recruiting with the functional areas. I have served as a key advisor and partner to top management, connecting their needs to an actionable development plan.

I am interested in relocating back to Houston for family reasons, and it appears I am unable to do that and remain with P&R. My references are excellent and will include a 360 review so you and a client company can be comfortable with my interactions up, down, and across. I will call you next week to follow up with you.

Thanks again!

David Heintzelman

Grace Fruit

1 Charlotte Way
Norman, NC 11111
704.555.5555

February 7, 20__

Ms. Eileen Dorn
Quality Assurance
1 Main Street, Suite A
Charlotte, NC 55555

Dear Ms. Dorn:

I understand you are recruiting for a private-sector liaison to work with the Virginia County expansion. My past accomplishments are closely aligned with this, and with my wealth of experience in navigating the civic waters, I believe my advisement can save you considerable time and money.

My enclosed resume illustrates my record of success in a complex environment of working through large corporations and the political and civic process. My most recent accomplishments are as follows:

- Drafted agreement and then led the implementation of a cooperative program designed to provide recycling services throughout the county.

- Negotiated a $24 million funding agreement resulting in the completion of 23 miles of Interstate 75 through Georgia.

- Developed and administered a $33 million disposal waste bond certificate for construction of master planned disposal facility in Fayetteville, North Carolina.

I will call you next Wednesday morning. Should you have any questions before I call, you may reach me at the number listed above.

Please keep my inquiry confidential, as I am just exploring alternatives, and please do not forward my materials to any employer without first discussing the particular opportunity with me.

Thank you very much for taking the time to review my resume and for your consideration. I look forward to our conversation.

Sincerely,

Grace Fruit

Kelly Garlow

110 Cumberland Way, Atlanta, GA 30303

December 5, 20__

Chris Ledford
Recruiting Specialist
South FL Recruiting
1 Boca Way
Boca Raton, FL 33678

Dear Mr. Ledford:

The *Palm Beach Post* recently displayed an advertisement for an administrative assistant, for which you are recruiting. As you will note from my enclosed resume, I have a very strong background in supporting attorneys and sales professionals. My administrative skills are well documented through my Certified Professional Secretary (CPS) rating, a credential which I enthusiastically maintain through continuous education and training.

Skilled at handling difficult situations, I fully understand the need to maintain confidentiality on sensitive issues and communicate with tact and diplomacy. I am widely recognized for my skills with many of the leading business software applications and all the Microsoft applications. My most recent typing speed was 88 words per minute with a 91 percent accuracy rate. I also speed-write and take shorthand, which is somewhat of an anomaly in today's highly technical workplace!

Mr. Ledford, I bring a record of loyalty, strong execution, and consistency in performance to every aspect of my work, and I am confident that my expertise would greatly benefit your client organization.

I will call you this Friday morning to discuss the opportunity in more detail.

Sincerely,

Kelly Garlow

Paula Taylor

3 Dallas Way
Grapevine, TX 75555
(972) 555-5555

April 24, 20__

Mr. Steven Rewter
430 Houston Way
Houston, TX 78444

Dear Mr. Rewter:

Throughout my career with Procter & Gamble, I have demonstrated expertise in efficient executive and office assistance. I have built a career specializing in dedicated support of my department's daily activities and long-term goals. I would like to do the same for your clients.

Comprehensive skills and an ability to work within many different levels of the corporate structure are exceptionally valuable in today's leaner organizations. As support positions need to take on more responsibility, the ability to handle a fast-paced environment and multitask is even more valuable.

Initiative, efficiency, an ability to "roll with the punches," and a short learning curve are the qualities of an administrative assistant who can step in and make an immediate contribution.

As a seasoned professional, I offer proven expertise in ever-changing schedules, written communications, confidential document administration, and time-sensitive assignments. I understand the complexities and procedures necessary to manage an executive's schedule and the daily operation of an office.

Mr. Rewter, I imagine there are many candidates who can *meet* your requirements. I will *exceed* your expectations. I know I can be an asset, making immediate contributions to your client companies. I will call you next week to discuss assignment possibilities.

Sincerely,

Paula Taylor

Gene Starew

101 Bobby Way • Detroit, MI 48221 • gs123@httryw.com

February 8, 20__

Paul Stanley
Stanley & Associates
1 Birmingham Street
Birmingham, MI 48207

Dear Mr. Stanley:

Michael Johnson mentioned to me that you specialize in the auto industry and that you might know of manufacturing companies looking for a vice president/general manager or director of operations. If so, please review my resume and consider introducing my credentials to them.

I took over the leadership at Plantronics five years ago. At that time, the plant was operating at a $1 million loss and realized low production rates (about 70% of potential capacity), too many downtime problems (18%), poorly trained staff, weak safety practices, high turnover, and lack of working morale between departments. I made the decision to retrain and empower our team and instilled a sense of accountability and continuous improvements into the system. Within the five years, we literally transformed the organization:

- The cost accounting analysis indicated we lowered our COGS by 7%, which went straight to the bottom line. We effectively kept costs the same while increasing productivity over 53%.
- We reduced overtime and kept it to a bare minimum by improving scheduling and accountability and reducing labor 2%, another component that went straight to the bottom line.

Mr. Stanley, we really did accomplish something special, and Michael was close enough to verify our success. I'd love to talk to you in more detail about what we did and how I might apply that success to a project or business unit of one of your clients.

Thanks, and I look forward to talking to you soon. I will call you next Tuesday to discuss it in more detail.

Sincerely,

Gene Starew

Becky Hiebert
909 Lawrenceville Drive, Overland Park, KS 11111
bholly@adl.com

June 15, 20__

Pam Wayne
Senior Recruiter, DRG
1111 Cinci Way
Dayton, OH 40000

Dear Ms. Wayne:

I understand that you recruit for sales professionals in the health-care and security industries. Should one of your clients desire a sales management professional with a history of leading outside B2B sales teams to top-tier sales performance, then we should discuss your client's objectives and what I have to offer.

My accomplishments include:

- A twelve-year record of ranking no lower than top three in any organization I have managed. Have won President's Club award in four of the past six years.
- Demonstrated expertise in assessing talent. Over past three years, have had less than 15% turnover, a key metric supporting our success: more turnover means rebuilding each time you hire someone new; less turnover means your team is meeting their objectives and building a business with legs to stand on.
- Instilling a teaching philosophy into the organization. Rather than tell the team to meet the results, I practice teaching them how to perform better, which has contributed to our results and low turnover.

Many candidates will represent these characteristics to you, but I promise I can support them with 360 references including those from my direct reports, my vice president, and customers.

I will call you Thursday to discuss any opportunities and perhaps seek some advice. Also, in my current role at ABC, I have used a recruiting firm for three hires over the past three years, so there might be an opportunity for you as a client source for me as well.

Sincerely,

Becky Hiebert

Tracie Russenberger
101 Waco Way, Waco TX 75555 tr@erc.org

July 2, 20__

Mr. John Caver
Caver and Associates
1 Addison Drive
Addison, TX 75240

Dear Mr. Caver:

Thank you so much for reaching out to me to discuss your client's position and your recruiting charter. Your e-mail indicated you are seeking to fill the executive director position for an undisclosed client in the banking industry.

I will call you Tuesday to discuss the opportunity. My understanding of the banking industry is that it is moving away from a passive sales environment and more toward one that demonstrates initiative to build the business. My retail background and track record are indeed a good fit for the banking business, considering that many of the drivers are transferable from my industry to that one.

Banking at the retail level is going through a transition and some of the legacy managers may not have the aggressive skills and tactics to shift from this passive to an active sales environment. With my professionalism in interacting with the industry and the sales performance I have driven, I believe I am a potentially excellent fit.

I will call you next week to discuss the opportunity. If you would like to set aside a half hour to an hour to talk, please drop me a note or call and let me know what works for you. Thanks!

Sincerely,

Tracie Russenberger

9
Networking

Without question, the most common, if not most effective, way people find out about and obtain new positions is through networking. The reason for this is not that so many opportunities come your way through networking. Actually, it's quite the opposite. You will uncover more opportunities through a site like Careerbuilder.com than cuts Tiger Woods has made since joining the PGA Tour. But here is a brilliant example of the difference between a cold application and an application made via networking (a true story).

Michael Davidson is a director for a Fortune 50 company in sales and marketing. He lost his position through a reduction in the workforce—it had nothing to do with a President's Club performance the year before the layoff. He networked with a colleague and learned about a new sales director position that was being created with an upstart firm in his industry. As they were creating the job description, the hiring vice president interviewed him over the phone, and two weeks later he flew to Charlotte for an interview.

Two days before his flight, he received a Careerbuilder.com Job Matches e-mail of new positions that matched the profile he'd created. One of those ads was for this position. He was offered the position a week later. The position was potentially identified both through networking and online, but his sponsorship got him the quick interview and he beat out the other applicants.

Same position, but networking and the sponsorship achieved through networking paid off.

Networking consists of people connecting, and when you connect with people, you begin to assemble your network. Once your network is in place, you will continue to make new contacts and communicate with established members. People in your network will provide advice, information, and support in helping you achieve your career goals and aspirations.

From most sources I have seen, networking accounts for up to 70 percent of the new opportunities uncovered.

So what is networking? Many people assume that they should call all the people they know personally and professionally and ask if they know of any companies that are hiring. A successful networker's approach is different. A successful networker starts by listing as many names as possible on a sheet of paper. Those names can include family members, relatives, friends, coworkers and managers (past and present), other industry contacts, and anyone else you know. The next step is to formulate a networking presentation.

Keep in mind that it need not address potential openings. In networking, the aim is to call your contacts to ask for career or industry advice. The point is that you position yourself not as a desperate job hunter but as a researcher. It is unrealistic to think that you will go far by asking people for advice like this:

> *Dave, thanks for taking some time to talk with me. My company is likely to lay people off next month and I was wondering if your company had any openings or if you know of any.*

This person hasn't told Dave what he does, has experience in, or wants to do. Dave is likely to respond by saying, "No, but I'll keep you in mind should I hear of anything." What do you think the odds are that Dave will contact this person again?

A better approach is to ask for personal or industry advice and work on developing the networking web:

> *Dave, Doug Matheson at the Richards Group suggested I give you a call. He and I have worked together for some time, and he mentioned that you work in finance and that you are the controller of Alcatel. I work in cost accounting and feel you may be able to offer some good career advice. I'd really appreciate some time. Could we get together for lunch sometime in the next week or so?*

The person has now asked for advice, not for a job. People are much more willing to help someone who has made them feel good about themselves or who appears to genuinely appreciate their help. This strategy can be approached in many ways. You can ask for job search advice (including resume or cover letter advice), overall career advice (as shown above), industry advice, key contacts, information about various companies/people/industries, and names of other people they may know.

It is important that the person you network through like you. When someone gives you a reference, it is a reflection on that person. People will not put themselves at personal or professional risk if they aren't confident that you will be a good reflection on them. Finally, send each person you speak with a thank-you letter. That courtesy will be remembered and lead to future contacts.

SIX DEGREES OF SEPARATION

In addition to traditional networking for opportunities, there is another very effective way to leverage networking in today's economy. Suppose you go to Monster.com and uncover a great opportunity with Bank of America, Intel, or a new company. Before blindly sending your resume and a brief cover letter to that company (or recruiter), immediately ask around and try to find a reference you can leverage to get to them. If you follow the rule of "six degrees of separation," there is a good chance you can ask around and get a personal introduction to the hiring manager.

The idea behind the six degrees of separation is that you may be no more than two or three people, or degrees, from getting connected to an employee at the company you are targeting. When you do, you have engineered a reference and network through the backdoor, or at least through a side door. Another terrific strategy to help you in this quest is to have your best references send in letters of recommendation to the hiring manager during the interview process. The determination you demonstrate by developing these references from your network will be perceived as the kind of determination you will demonstrate on the job. Companies desperately need good employees. Sell yourself as one of those employees, and most companies will find a place for you.

A client of mine, Grace, was looking to find a position with Comerica Bank. The company's Web site had a posting for a position they wanted filled that was located in Atlanta. But how do you avoid being batched in the plethora of applicants these companies receive for each posting, especially in today's economy?

Here is what we did: we worked with the candidate to see if she knew *anyone* at Comerica. We researched and learned that many former Wachovia executives worked at Comerica, as well as former Citigroup managers. After a few days of asking around, it turned out that Grace's former colleague at Wachovia knew a vice president at Comerica. So we called her and got the name of her former vice president. Grace called the vice president in Atlanta, and he actually picked up the phone, in part because Grace called before hours, when things were slow, and waited until he answered the phone, rather than leaving a voicemail.

Grace gave him a quick "elevator pitch" of her background and what her goals were, and the vice president referred her to that region's vice president. Grace reached that vice president and by then had a few names to drop, positioning herself as a referred candidate. The new vice president had Grace get in touch with a human resources recruiter, and a few weeks later Grace secured an interview and a position.

That whole networking exercise took just two days but enabled Grace to scoop hundreds of other candidates. You, too, should think of creative ways to network internally.

Michelle Bristow

1111 Tampa Road • Oldsmar, FL 33556 • mb@yahaa.com • 813-555-1212

Debbie Davis
Director of Operations
Wireless Co., Inc.
ddavis@wc.com

Dear Ms. Davis:

Lisa Williams suggested I contact you, and I believe she mentioned me to you as well. Lisa told me how long you have led the sales organization for WC, and I believe you would be a good person from whom to seek advice.

Lisa said that you began your career in sales as an individual contributor sales representative in the B2B arena, worked your way up to sales management, and are now the director of sales for the region. I am currently a two-year-running top sales performer as an individual contributor and am interested in moving up in management, allowing for a greater impact on the organization as a whole and furthering my own career and development.

Can we schedule time to talk next week for 20 to 30 minutes? I would like to seek general advice from you, as well as follow up on the sales manager position Lisa mentioned to me to see if there is potential for a mutual fit.

Thanks and have a great day!

Michelle Bristow

David Ryan

2202 Mary Way
Baltimore, MD 01001
Daveryan@soulter.com
301 555 0000

Dawn E. McCarter
VP of Merchandising
The Gap

Dear Ms. McCarter:

I was visiting New York recently and ran into a friend from college, Steve Taylor, who works with you at The Gap. Steve told me about some of your career highlights while at The Gap:

- ▣ Transitioned from spokesperson and model to marketing executive, the first time anyone has made that transition in the fashion industry, as far as he is aware.
- ▣ Successfully marketed the SuperDave campaign for young men's attire.
- ▣ Created a marketing initiative to double market share in Austin with University of Texas students and increase sales of ladieswear.
- ▣ Managed creative control of the ultra-soft blue "Every-Wear" unisex top.
- ▣ Recognized as the top marketing executive in 2007 by *Marketing Age* magazine.

This spring, my daughter is graduating from Michigan State University in marketing, and she is very interested in the fashion industry. She will be contacting you to ask for some advice and to explore any opportunities at your company.

Thanks again, and please expect Tracie Ryan's call and e-mail.

Sincerely,

David Ryan

Grace Fruit
gfruit@usafinance.net
704 555 0000

Eileen Dorn
Vice President, Operations
Comerica Bank, Chicago, IL

Dear Ms. Dorn:

Tracie Gusola, a colleague of mine at USA Finance, said she spoke with you last week at the ITF conference in Atlanta. She was quite impressed with the things you had to say and with your credentials. She is also aware that I am pursuing a career in finance and banking and insisted I contact you to seek advice.

With the growth it is realizing right now, including aggressive expansion in Alabama, Texas, and New Mexico, Comerica needs strong sales and operations leadership. The trend for most banking retailers is assuming just that, a more aggressive retail approach, with more initiative and effort put into servicing customers and obtaining more business share from each customer.

My accomplishments include encouraging very strong sales teams, high morale, low turnover, and, in general, a very energetic and fun environment.

I will call you next Tuesday at 9 a.m., but if that is not a convenient time for you, please drop me a quick note with an alternative. I really look forward to speaking with you next week.

Thanks again,

Grace Fruit

Patrick Workley
pworkley@tdic.org
972 555 0000

Kevin Alcorn
IT Call Center Manager
PB&R Corporation, Dallas, TX

Dear Mr. Alcorn:

A mutual friend of ours, Bob Ferguson, suggested I contact you. I am currently living in Houston but am moving to Dallas in a few weeks, for certain, and there is a good chance I will not be continuing to work for NCR when I relocate.

I have been looking at IT as a prospective employer and was excited when Bob told me he knew you. IT is an attractive company for me to target for the following reasons:

- IT tends to be more customer focused than many other companies in the industry.
- The culture at IT is appealing. It seems to be the Southwest Airlines of the technology infrastructure industry: work hard, but play hard and make the work fun, too.
- While the market has been fairly flat, particularly in this industry, IT has experienced double-digit top-line revenue growth and growth in share value.
- The WIMAX initiative IT is pursuing will enable true competitive differentiation.

I have led inside support teams and run the highest proficiency ratings in the past two years. May we set up a time next week to discuss whether there is a mutual fit? Also, I will be in Dallas the week of March 12. If you are in town that week, I could take you to lunch. Even if there presently is no opportunity for me at IT, I'd love to get some inside advice with respect to the industry climate in Dallas.

Thanks, Mr. Alcorn.

Sincerely,

Patrick Workley

Elsie Coxon
Elsie.coxon@fordmot.com
443 555 0000

Alice Scarpitti
Director, Customer Service
Plantronics, Newport, DE

Dear Ms. Scarpitti:

Your son Steve and I went to school together at the University of Delaware. When I was in Baltimore last week, Steve and I had lunch, and he suggested I contact you.

For the two years since we left school, I have been a CSR with Eaglein in Cherry Hill. The position has been rewarding, and I have learned much about the industry and how to efficiently service customers, ensuring their satisfaction while staying on the proper call counts.

In the past year, of the 65 CSRs in our center, I have led in overall satisfaction according to postcall surveys. I have also led the call center in shortest time per call, thus enabling more customers to be serviced per shift. In addition, whenever new CSRs are hired, I am selected as the trainer for them. I like Eaglein, and they have told me that I am next in line for a leadership position. However, the organization is really not growing.

Steve mentioned your role with Plantronics and encouraged me to contact you. The prospect of joining a growing organization is very exciting.

May we set up some time to speak over the next week? I will follow this up with a call to you late Friday morning. Thanks, Ms. Scarpitti.

Sincerely,

Elsie Coxon

Kevin Kahlden
K2@tsu.com
512 555 0000

Paul Rigley
Recruitment Advisor
Regusten Products, Inc.
New York, NY 10001

Dear Mr. Rigley:

Zach Stirling, the group manager for consumer goods in Cincinnati, informed me of your search for a director of enterprise solutions. Zach was a direct report of mine from 2005 to 2007. At that time our group was considered the "whiz kid" group within TSU. The product launches we delivered included the KidBox and Emerlin Wizard.

The success of our product launches was a direct reflection of the team I led, which included Zach. Things are good at TSU, but there is a reason for my inquiry. TSU has become a large and less nimble organization than when I joined eight years ago. We've had much success, but it has come with a price.

From what Zach has shared with me, Regusten is that more dynamic, quick-to-react-and-develop company we once were. For that reason—and for the creativity and direct impact on the organization it allows—Regusten is the company I am interested in learning more about and possibly joining.

I will call you next Wednesday morning to discuss this in more detail. I have also attached my resume.

Thanks in advance for your consideration.

Kevin Kahlden

Talitha Schmidt
Talitha@mwn.com
940 555 0000

Rose Lennon
Director of Human Resources
Fastener Lights Inc.
Los Angeles, CA

Dear Ms. Lennon:

I really enjoyed speaking with you on that flight from Dallas to Los Angeles a little over a year ago. I am sure you fly all the time, but hopefully you recall a great conversation about business and your career while our takeoff was delayed due to that ice storm in Dallas. You gave me your card and suggested I contact you when I graduated from USC.

I did graduate and began working with Hardon International. However, my studies in psychology and interest in the human development side of business have prompted me to get back in touch with you. I remember your philosophy on leading teams, assessing talent in recruitment, and training.

At Hardon, my role has been as a marketing coordinator. Three interns report to me on several projects, and, overall, things are healthy here. However, I do think that the human development discipline is my calling.

May we get together sometime this month? I am first and foremost asking for industry advice from someone who has the drive, energy, personality, and experience I admire. Were there to be any opportunities at Fastener, I'd love to discuss those as well.

Thanks, Rose!

Talitha

Greg Starr
Gregs@juonr.com
404 555 0000

Mike Jackson
Vice President of Operations
Rooparm Industries

Dear Mr. Jackson:

You and I had a brief meeting at the CES show in Las Vegas earlier this year. When we spoke, we discussed WIMAX access for the Emerlin product and the impact that could have on the industry. At the time, you were very interested in the viability of the offering and its readiness for the market. You also suggested we stay in touch.

Do you have any time over the next couple weeks to meet face-to-face—perhaps have lunch or get a coffee for a few minutes? We have made some exciting headway in some key areas, having completed the creative part of the product offer. Now it's up to sales and distribution to have their way. The thought of exploring an opportunity that would enable more creativity and a contribution to the team developing the ZCube is intriguing.

Considering the leadership contribution I made on the Emerlin product offer, I have some very exciting ideas on offer development. I am very interested in learning more about the direction Rooparm is taking and your thoughts on the industry in general.

I will give you a call Thursday to discuss the business, which, at a minimum, will be mutually beneficial, to compare notes.

Sincerely,

Greg Starr

Mark Riley
mriley@chase.net

Doug Matheson
Vice President of Operations
SS Industries

Dear Mr. Matheson:

It was a pleasure to meet with you this morning for breakfast. I realize how busy you are, and I appreciate the time you took out of your schedule. I am very excited about the new product development in anti-inflammatory drugs on the horizon and the magnitude of the effect they could have on today's illnesses.

The work in this area that Jennifer London is leading at PARC Research fits in well with the orthopedic research and sports rehabilitation work I have completed. As you said, I think there is a potentially good fit here. I will be contacting Jennifer by the end of the week.

You mentioned you would call her as well. If you could do that before I connect with her, it might help her be more receptive to my cold call.

Thanks again for meeting me this morning. I'll give you a call next week to let you know what happened.

Best regards!

Mark Riley
404 555 0000

Marybeth Rouse
mbrouse@whitney.net
949 555 0000

Tracie Gusola
Vice President, Operations
Comerica Bank, Chicago, IL

Dear Ms. Gusola:

Thank you so much for speaking with me yesterday. After four years, I was not sure you would remember me, since our paths did not cross all that often.

I am so glad you did and that you recalled our then-new Outreach Program to drive mortgage sales.

As I mentioned to you earlier, I am reentering the workforce after taking the last two years off for the birth of my child.

You asked me to recap some career highlights for you in writing:

- Led sales organization of new outbound sales initiative Outreach through 47 bank locations and 30 employees.
- Increased share of mortgage to checking accounts from 0.9% to 4% in a two-year period, considered a very strong success within the corporation.
- Hired the three team leaders for this initiative; all of them are still with the company and two have since been promoted.

I thank you in advance for anything you can do to put me in touch with Tom Porter and anyone else you think would be beneficial.

Thanks again, Tracie!

Marybeth Rouse

SAMUEL HARDEN

1 Madison Way, Irvine, CA 91111 949.555.1111
cd@qway.net

June 21, 20__

Ms. Jane Stoney
Senior Vice President, Cocoa Corporation
999 John Carpenter Freeway
Las Colinas, TX 72222

Dear Jane:

I have left you a voicemail, but I wanted to follow up via e-mail as well. I am currently the controller for the consumer division for Snacks LTD., in Irvine, California. I am planning to move from California to Texas by the end of the year (am able to now) and thought of you.

Several disciplines within our respective corporations have commonalities. As a financial officer, I have had many interactions and touch each discipline within the organization. What we have accomplished over the last two years is nothing short of remarkable, having improved our division from losing about $1.7 million a year to being $1.3million in the black this year (trend). To effect that change, my group's role was to do the following:

- ▣ Took the initiative to work with marketing, the buyers, and the sales organization to improve each financial lever in the business. This included working with marketing on more targeted promotional efforts and improved co-op fund use.
- ▣ On the sales side, I or my assistant controller joined their group calls every other week to update them on financial performance and work to tweak the cost levers of payroll and labor, reduce returns, and turn around our inventory more quickly.
- ▣ On the buying side, we bought more strategically and drastically reduced the amount of slow-moving inventory.

Given the similarities in our businesses, I bet there are significant benefits worth exploring if I were to join Cocoa. While I know this is outside your discipline, I would like to speak with you to simply better understand your corporate structure as well as the Dallas area.

I will call you later in the week. Thanks, Jane.

Sincerely,

Samuel Harden

Renee Powers

222 Norfolk Way, Richmond, VA 44444 ☐ 804 555 0000 ☐ rpowers@blbg.net

April 19, 20___

William Blount
Director of Human Resources
14 Dallas Parkway
Highland Park, TX 75000

Dear Mr. Blount:

We met in January at the Recruiting and Hiring Expo in San Antonio. You gave me your card and suggested I contact you if I were to consider moving to Dallas from Houston.

I am going to be moving to Dallas in June and would love to speak with you. When we met, I found that we think very much alike in our approach to hiring and how to better assess talent, in any discipline. I am quite skilled at behavioral interviewing and have seen the value hiring right up front creates within an organization:

❖ Reduced turnover in the division I supported helped us reach a higher level of productivity. In sales, we achieved a higher percentage-to-target win, and two marketing managers I helped recruit went on to win national awards of excellence.

I believe, passionately, that the line-level managers, whom I support and recruit for, are my customers, and I make every effort to help them find the best people. In many cases, I mined for candidates and talked a reluctant candidate who was not job searching into meeting with us. He did end up joining us and is a top performer.

Of course, I can provide excellent references to support this list of my contributions.

If nothing else, I would love some advice from you, both professionally and on my move to Dallas.

I am looking forward to speaking with you soon.

Sincerely,

Renee Powers

10
Target Companies Directly

Aren't there one or two companies you've always been interested in working for? Ideally, you may know someone who will introduce you to key contacts there or inform you of future openings. The best way to get introduced to a targeted company is to have a current employee personally introduce you or make an introductory phone call for you. You could make the introduction and reference the employee you know.

We'll get into this later, but if you don't know anyone at a targeted company, a recruiter may be a good source of contact for you, even if it involves no job order for him or her. You could send an unsolicited resume, but the likelihood of this working is low. Most large-profile companies receive thousands of resumes a year, and few are acted on. Corporate recruiters Jackie Larson and Cheri Comstock, authors of *The New Rules of the Job Search Game* (Adams Media, 1994), don't take mass-mailed resumes very seriously. Part of the problem is that too many resumes are written as past job descriptions and are not customized to a targeted position. Conrad Lee, a retained Boca Raton recruiter, believes "information is the most important thing in contacting companies directly. Don't call just one person in the company and feel that is sufficient. That person may have their own job insecurities or be on a performance improvement plan. You should contact five to ten people and only then can you say you contacted that company directly." New job search strategies all suggest targeting a select few of smaller companies (under 750 employees, as larger companies are still downsizing) intensely rather than blanketing a thousand generically.

Contacting the head of your functional specialty in that company is a good start. Is it hard? Of course. You're facing rejection, probably feeling like you're bothering busy people, begging, maybe even feeling inferior. Would you feel inferior if you were calling hotels and ticket agencies for Super Bowl information? Of course not. What if someone can't help you? You just get back on the phone until you achieve your goal. These contacts should be approached the same way.

You have a great product to sell—yourself. Position yourself as someone of value and as a product that can contribute to the target company. The key is to position yourself for individual situations. This requires specialized letters, resumes, and strategies tailored for each situation. One trick is to call the company you are targeting and try to get the name of the person in charge of the department where you would like to work. If you don't know, call the receptionist and ask her or him who that is and perhaps the name of a vendor or two (such as an accounting firm or ad agency) and then check the company Web site for the latest company news. Now you have something interesting to talk about when you reach the hiring manager.

INCREASE YOUR ODDS: GET IN

There are two different things you need to try to do to increase your odds in contacting companies directly. The first is to network your way internally to the decision maker. The second is to get an internal reference.

With small companies this can be difficult, but not with large Fortune 1000 companies. If you circulate and network effectively, you should be no more than two or three degrees from any major company employer, particularly if you're grounded in that industry.

Create a "family tree" of relationships you have with others and map out each one by industry. Start asking around for people who work for your targeted company or an affiliate (key customer, strategic partner, vendor) of that company. Keep looking. If you come up empty, go to a local restaurant for lunch or a happy-hour spot that is near their office. Be subtle and ask around. You will find someone. Strike up a neutral conversation and then offer to treat a person to lunch in return for some fact-finding information. If they like you, they will in almost all cases refer you internally. You've scored. An internal reference is worth more than any other kind of reference.

KATHLEEN MCCOY

1 Melbourne Way, Denver, CO 33333 303.555.1111
ts@qway.net

October 2, 20__

Dr. Steven Porter
1 Pikes Peak, Colorado Springs, CO 00000

Dear Dr. Porter:

One of your patients of many years, Mary Rouse, suggested I contact you. She informed me that you were seeking an additional dental hygienist for your growing practice, and she was aware that I am a recent graduate ready to begin my career in the field.

I have interned at a local dentist's office near school and acquired many skills that will make my learning curve short and my ability to "hit the ground running" a reality. I provided technical assistance and support for the two dentists in this office during dental examinations and procedures, according to established protocols. I prepared instruments and treatment materials, obtained radiographic images and dental impressions, and provided patients with general information and instruction about care. I even helped one or two with their insurance claims!

I have attached my resume, and I am very interested in learning more about this opportunity and exploring a potential fit. I will call you Thursday to discuss the opportunity in more detail.

Thanks in advance for your time and consideration.

Sincerely,

Kathleen McCoy

TRIP COPY
1 Madison Way, Irvine, CA 91111
tc@qway.net

February 10, 20__

Ms. Michelle Bristow
Vice President, Human Resources, Nokia
999 John Carpenter Freeway
Las Colinas, TX 72222

Dear Ms. Bristow:

I understand Nokia is now looking for a director of human resources to lead the recruiting efforts for your North America operation. Understanding the real needs of the functional managers, taking that charter, and teaching the recruiting organization how to spot and assess that talent and get it right the first time are critical to making this functionperform well. Whoever fills this position must recognize that his or her internal customer is the line-level manager needing a skilled employee.

Considering that people are a company's biggest asset, this position is a vital one. When companies or even sports teams succeed or fail, it invariably comes down to people and leadership. I truly believe this, and can support it with my track record and references from peers and from people who have reported to me and to whom I have reported.

If you believe that people are the differentiator, then I am certain I can help. As human resources director for a Fortune 500 company in the area, I have introduced new practices to help my company better attract, assess, and recruit more talented people. Our turnover rate since these new programs were instituted has been over 30% below historical average; 90% of the new hires we made at XYZ are still with us two years into their tenure.

I am confident that I can help build on Nokia's foundation. I will call you Tuesday to see if we might schedule a meeting to learn more about one another. Thank you for your time and consideration, and I look forward to our conversation.

Sincerely,

Trip Copy

Dawn P.G. McCarter

101 Longhorn Way, Dallas, TX 75240 ☐ 972 555 0000 ☐ dawnpgmccarter@stwain.com

October 24, 20___

Michael M. Master
IMS Corporation
2 Chai Way
Hilton Head, SC 75240

Dear Mr. Master:

I am writing at the recommendation of our mutual acquaintance, Robert Seger, contributor to *About Last Night*, who suggested I contact you concerning the new direction IMS is taking. Based on what Robert shared with me, I understand that your group is taking a sharp turn toward building the B2C channel to increase that channel's performance by a factor of two to three over the next two years. In order to achieve this, bringing on accomplished leadership will be critical.

The ability to assess talent in building the team, and then effectively drive performance using a team-spirited and positive approach, is critical. Here are some career highlights that demonstrate my close alignment with those goals:

- ☐ Established myself as the "The Dawn McCarter of Sprint," whereby I was promoted to director in the number one market after two successive promotions three years into my employment there. Have finished no lower than number two of 28-plus directors nationwide each year since 1999.
- ☐ Affected a sales increase by a factor of 4 to 5 in the University of Texas market by prompting young students to buy in the hope of being with me or like me.
- ☐ At two Pinnacle Club events, took the lead on entertainment, performing *The Dawn McCarter Show*, featuring a selection of songs by Shania Twain, in which my voice and appearance are very much like those of the pop star.
- ☐ Effectively and eagerly use alliteration as means to communicate key messages to create fun and positive e-mails that motivate partners and team members.
- ☐ Nearly recovered from two IDPs through concerted effort, attention to detail, and change in behavior.

These skills and accomplishments appear to fit in well with the new direction IMS is taking. If IMS is serious about this soft-performing channel breaking out this year, strong and experienced leadership is critical. Let's set up some time to talk about this in more detail, even if we consider it exploratory.

I will call you Friday morning to talk, and maybe we can set up a time to meet early next month. Feel free to give me a call anytime as well. Have a great week!

Sincerely,

Dawn P.G. McCarter

Marcos Cancel

1 PR Way, Puerto Rico 00000
(487) 555-5555

January 29, 20___

Carolyn Kellenberger, Board of Directors
St. Michael's Elementary School
9911 Fairfield
Livonia, MI 48022

Dear Ms. Kellenberger:

I understand you are seeking a Spanish teacher for your elementary school. I have recently moved to the Detroit area from Puerto Rico and am very interested in teaching Spanish at these grade levels.

I had a brief conversation with Mary Anne last week and she shared with me some of the objectives and key skill areas you are seeking to fill.

My goals and vision for St. Michael's are:

1. To support the Catholic development and spirit of teaching.
2. To teach the children not just how to speak Spanish but how to think in Spanish as well.
3. To create a fun environment in which the students are motivated and encouraged to learn.
4. To achieve a 100% passing rate for all students, and to best prepare the students for the future in an ever-shrinking world of global economics and politics.

Some of the strengths I can bring to this position are:

- Taught English in Puerto Rico and achieved the highest passing rates in the district.
- Established great relationships with parents of students and excellent communication with them on developmental opportunities for the students, and created a joint plan for success.
- Possess a desire to work with peer teachers, the school principal, the school board, and the PTA.

Mary Anne helped me submit my application to the board last week, and I will give you a call Wednesday to discuss this in more detail.

Sincerely,

Marcos Cancel

PATRICIA CAPIZZI   Beach Road One, Miami, Florida 33333 ■ (954) 555-0000

March 19, 20___

Mike Gusola
ARP Engineering
1 Castle Hill Drive
Castle Hills, TX 75556

Dear Mr. Gusola:

I am graduating from Florida Atlantic University with a degree in electrical engineering in the spring.
My ideas about design and my depth of experience are above the norm for graduates in this program.
In the interest of working with ARP, I am enclosing my resume for your consideration.

I worked part-time during the school year and full-time during my semester off at the Pratt Whitney
facility in Boynton Beach. My background working for PW on large development projects, coupled
with my formal education, makes me an excellent candidate for employment with ARP.

I am familiar with ARP and its vast array of high-tech projects including the design and construction
of the new internal air combustion J3500 engine. Many of ARP's major projects are sponsored by the
Department of Defense. I am comfortable working within the tangle of government red tape and
have already received security clearance.

ARP employs professionals who are distinguished graduates. Your reputation is outstanding within
the industry. Considering my academic record (top 5% of my class) and long-standing internship
with PW, I should be able to fit in with this great collection of engineering talent.

I will call you next Tuesday to discuss this in more detail. Also, you can count on me providing
strong references from FAU and PW, along with my level 2 security clearance.

Sincerely,

Patricia Capizzi

Patrick Workley

1 Caroline Way ▪ Christopher, TX 75555 ▪ pw@tt.org

April 27, 20__

Mr. Bob Ferguson
Senior Editor, S&S
14 Park Avenue
New York, NY 11111

Dear Mr. Ferguson:

I really appreciate the time you spent with me on the phone this morning. As I am now rejoining the workforce after a hiatus during which my two children were born, I am excited about getting back in the game and getting off the sidelines.

You asked me to send you a quick note highlighting some of my accomplishments and what I am interested in doing. Here are some highlights and a recap of some of the things we discussed this morning:

- Worked in publishing industry with two top-five publishers for eight years, from 1995 to 2003.
- Was the sponsoring editor for 1999's *Bright Dawn Eyes*, a manuscript two publishers passed on that reached number 14 on the *New York Times* bestseller fiction list.
- Edited a three-book series on child development; each book sold over 250,000 copies within its first two years in print.

While enjoying my time off, I remained an avid reader. I read at least twenty works of fiction a year, plus I subscribe to several periodicals. I miss the work and am very excited to return to a field about which I am passionate.

I will take you up on your offer to get together for lunch in the next couple weeks. I will call Deanne on Monday to set up a time.

Thank you again for the consideration you have given me. I appreciate all your assistance, and will let you know how my search progresses.

Best regards,

Patrick Workley

Chris Zach

1111 Chicago Road • Norstar, IL 44444 • cz@yahaa.com • 213-555-1212

December 1, 20__

Randy Taview
Director of Operations
Jupiter Manufacturing Inc.
taview@jmi.com

Dear Mr. Taview:

Please accept this letter in application for the posting of a public sector executive with your organization.

Since my early retirement from Ford Motor Company a few months ago, I have had my fill of retirement living and miss working and the interaction with colleagues and clients, the negotiations, and the challenge of overcoming obstacles to win.

For 26 years, I was with General Motors and then Ford Motor Company, and I spent a bulk of that time bridging the corporate objectives with government regulations and managing the ensuing complications, calling on exceptional interpersonal skills with public-sector leaders and our line-level managers.

At Ford, when there was a regulatory problem, I was always the liaison called to the scene. I have contacts at all government levels, local and state (Michigan, Illinois, and Ohio) as well as federal, and I have proven my ability to navigate through public concerns and corporate objectives.

I offer you a unique combination of tactical and strategic experience, strong interpersonal communications ability, and industry knowledge, which will help you immeasurably in your public relations efforts. Could we meet to discuss the ways in which I might enhance your customer satisfaction levels? I eagerly await a call from you to schedule a time for us to speak.

Thank you for your time and consideration of my qualifications.

Sincerely,

Chris Zach

Alice Scarpitti
111 Delaware Road, Forth, DE 10101 804-555-4444

January 10, 20___

Mr. David Watsky
Watsky and Associates
90 Stemmons Freeway, Suite 100
Dallas, TX 75200

RE: **Legal Assistant Position**

Dear Mr. Watsky:

I recently graduated from Dallas Community College with certification as a paralegal and legal assistant. Eager to use my new skills, I have been conducting job-related research at the Career Center on campus, and there I learned about the work your firm has done with the college over the years. Please accept my enclosed resume, as I am pursuing a legal assistant position in this area and within your legal specialty.

My background is centered on legal writing, and I am quite adept at writing, proofing briefs, and associated research. At DCC, I assisted the research librarian at the college library. During prior experience as a secretary, I composed correspondence, researched and compiled client files, and analyzed information for the vice president and principal. I look forward to the opportunity to put these skills and my newly earned certification to work for you.

My education and experience and the skills I am passionate about will serve Watsky and Associates well. I believe I would be equally rewarded by the experience I would receive in your law office. Thank you for your time and consideration of my qualifications; I look forward to speaking with you soon. I will call you Wednesday to discuss the direction your firm is taking and to explore a potential fit.

Respectfully,

Alice Scarpitti

Alex White
1 Carrollton Way, Carrollton, TX 75243   alexwhite@waret.com   214 555 0000

March 12, 20__

John Caver
Caver and Associates
jc@ca.net

Dear Mr. Caver:

Danny Plare suggested I contact you regarding an architect position you are seeking to fill. Please accept this letter and the enclosed resume as an application for a position with you. Danny has always spoken highly of you, and your firm has established itself as the leader in industrial development in the state of Texas.

My enclosed resume details the skills and accomplishments I have in design within the manufacturing and industrial industries. You can see I have:

- Considerable experience in the field of construction and architecture combined with a formal education.

- A proven record of success achieved through creativity, commitment, attention to detail, and a belief in consistent execution of the fundamentals.

- Experience working on three medium- and large-sized Fortune 500 development projects in the manufacturing arena.

I would like to meet with you to discuss whether there might be a potential fit for both of us and will call you Thursday to arrange a meeting. If you have any questions or want to talk, feel free to contact me as well.

Thanks, and I look forward to speaking with you soon.

Sincerely,

Alex White

CAMERON DAY

1 Madison Way, Irvine, CA 91111 949.555.1111
cd@qway.net

February 10, 20__

Ms. Tiffany Coal
Vice President, Human Resources, Startac
999 John Carpenter Freeway
Las Colinas, TX 72222

Dear Ms. Coal:

Please accept this letter and accompanying resume to support my interest in applying for a receptionist position with your company.

My resume illustrates the experience I have in the administrative area, which includes:

- Over seven years' experience as a receptionist at two Fortune 1000 companies, demonstrating stability within these professional environments.

- Experience and comfort working in a high-pressure and fast-paced environment.

- Experience working with the latest NT phone systems and PBX switch centers.

- Excellent references from my two most recent employers. I left the last employer when we moved from California to Texas late last year.

Please take a look at my resume. I would like to meet with you to discuss how effectively I can contribute. I will call you Friday morning to discuss the opportunity. Should you have any questions before then, feel free to give me a call or drop me an e-mail.

Sincerely,

Cameron Day

Lisa Williams

1 PR Way, Puerto Rico 00000
(487) 555-5555

May 19, 20__

Taylor Dawton
PeteTrade Financial
16111 Blue Ridge Circle
Palm Beach, FL 33440

Dear Mr. Dawton:

After contributing to the growth and success of Fidelity Services for over a decade, I am seeking new challenges with an enterprising company in need of someone with exceptional planning, leadership, and analytical qualities. One of your colleagues, Debbie Davis, and I met for lunch earlier this week in Tampa and she recommended that I contact you regarding prospective opportunities in your department.

My experience encompasses all aspects of sales development, strategic planning, account planning, full P&L management, tax planning, and budgeting. My ability to analyze needs and develop unique programs designed to yield a profitable outcome are my strongest skills.

I excel at financial modeling and resolving complex situations in order to generate investment/costing details for new business ventures. I am technologically proficient, with direct experience in remittance, imaging, and systems design and development. My record of achievements is exemplary, as I have successfully directed and managed complex assignments while meeting or exceeding anticipated scheduling and budgetary projections.

Characterized by others as visionary and decisive, I develop intuitive solutions and offer strategies to quickly effect change and improvement. I am equally at ease working as a team member or independently, and enjoy a leadership role where I can foster motivational and mentoring relationships with colleagues and subordinates.

I am most interested in an opportunity where I can provide strong corporate leadership and vision. Debbie said so many complimentary things about you, I am really quite anxious to meet you face-to-face. I will call you next Monday to secure a date on your calendar.

Best regards,

Lisa Williams

Maria Lane

1 Maryland Way, Baltimore, MD 00000
(301) 555-5555

January 29, 20__

Patrick Dudash
9911 Fairfield
Livonia, MI 48022

Dear Mr. Dudash:

I read in *Health Journal* that Fairfield General was successful in securing the federal grant for support in cancer cell research. You were quoted on the hospital's expansion and need for talented staff to support the research endeavor.

The timing for the grant and your expansion couldn't be better. I am relocating back to the Detroit area next month and would be honored to be considered a candidate to help this cause. With over 10 years' experience as an oncologist and then cell research director at Johns Hopkins in Ohio, I believe my qualifications and experience align well with what you are seeking.

When I came on board at Johns Hopkins, there were numerous organizational challenges to be tackled. Foremost among them was the need to set proper expectations relative to our grants and determine aggressive yet attainable schedules for our team to deliver and by which to manage closely. We achieved several breakthroughs, and overall our program was a success and our funding was renewed for another two years.

While this is but one of the accomplishments highlighted on my enclosed resume, I believe it speaks to my effectiveness in a leadership role while maintaining my focus on navigating the political landscape. My staff would describe me as compassionate and good-natured, but they are also quick to acknowledge my abilities in assessing a complex situation for what it is and implementing swift measures to resolve any issues. I am confident that I can lead your team to similar success.

I will call you next Wednesday to discuss this in more detail.

Sincerely,

Maria Lane

Rasheen Ashad

1 Houston Drive, Houston, TX 77777 832.555.1111 ra@watg.org

August 1, 20__

Mr. Isaiah Wallace
Vice President, The Limited Corporation
1 Dublin Drive
Dublin, OH 44444

Dear Mr. Wallace:

Michelle Bristow, a former district manager for the Victoria's Secret fragrance channel, and I have worked together for nearly two years, and she suggested that I contact you, as you are recruiting a regional manager for the men's clothing channel Express for Men.

My fourteen-year career includes experience with Bed, Bath and Beyond and Bebe, where I was responsible for the buying and merchandising functions for ready-to-wear departments and stores. I had management responsibility for 125 stores and over $130 million in top-line revenue annually. My specific skills include performance management within the stores and of district managers, and assessing talent on the front end of recruiting.

The following accomplishments are representative of the abilities I can bring to The Limited:

- Achievement of optimally eight times inventory turnover and 14% profit through performance management techniques and aggressive sales techniques, as well as operational management through optimized scheduling and cost controls.

- Top regional performance within both best-in-class retailers with which I have led, with verifiable performance statistics.

- Most distinguished in talent assessment and development: by far, the lowest district manager turnover in the last two years; developed all three current peer regional directors promoted from district manager.

- Set pace for "soft skills" development within field organization companywide: store visits, coaching, performance management, how to develop managers, and determining whether to develop or release team members.

As an industry veteran, I have long respected The Limited for its fashion leadership, value orientation, and visual merchandising presentation. I'd like to bring my expertise and commitment to excellence to The Limited. I look forward to meeting with you to discuss the ways in which I can contribute to the continuing success of your dynamic management team.

Sincerely,

Rasheen Ashad

Don Henlye

1 Moon Drive, Houston, TX 77777 832.555.1111 dh@tygle.net

March 1, 20___

Helen Kramer
Chief People Development Officer
Western Alliance Corporation
1 Okeechobee, West Palm Beach, FL 33409

Response for Financial Specialist

Dear Ms. Kramer:

I am responding to the posting for a financial specialist in the tax arena that is on the *Palm Beach Post* site this week. My accomplishments and areas of expertise are outlined on the enclosed resume.

Here are some brief career highlights that closely align with what you are looking for based on the posting:

- Graduate of University of Florida with accounting degree; graduated in top 20% of class
- Extracurricular work with H&R Block on tax preparation each tax season for past five years
- Primary position with Easton Corporation for past six years in cost accounting area for manufacturing

I am exploring opportunities not only in the tax field, but also in other management areas such as general accounting, financial services, and recruiting of accounting or financial management personnel. At Easton I had the least employee turnover of any business unit and the highest productivity recorded within our discipline.

I would welcome the opportunity to talk to you in more detail about the prospect of joining this accomplished leadership team. I'll give you a call next Tuesday to discuss your objectives and direction. I look forward to our conversation.

Sincerely,

Don Henlye

TAMMY SHANAHAN

1 Melbourne Way, Denver, CO 33333 303.555.1111
ts@qway.net

February 10, 20___

Ms. Kathleen McCoy
Vice President, Kijo Corporation
1 Pikes Peak, CO Springs, CO 00000

Dear Ms. McCoy:

I am new to the Denver/Springs area, and your name has come up in several conversations recently. As a newcomer to the area, I have been asking people if they know of any interior design companies with an outstanding reputation and premier client base. Since I won't settle for joining a firm of any less stature, perhaps you could give me fifteen minutes of your time to discuss your future direction and a potential fit.

My experience includes team design and floor plan projects for both residential and commercial buildings. I spent the last three years with Jane Dewy Designs in Orlando, Florida, one of the most prestigious design firms in the state. Among the award-winning projects I was a part of, I was most proud of these two:

- The Palace Tower renovation, a 109,000-square-foot medium-rise office building in the central commerce area in Orlando, with a gorgeous open-air atrium. I'd love to show you some design sketches and pictures of this.

- Waterfront Towers (ironically, not near any water) in downtown, a residential twelve-story new co-op development. I was commissioned to design the two model units and ended up designing four sold units as a result.

I read that you are bidding on several new projects, including the new Burgess Development residential building and Qwest's new regional headquarters in Castle Rock. I would love to work on these projects with you and am certain my experience would add a lot of value. I am not interested in ever owning my own firm; the creative side is much more my passion than the administrative functions that accompany owning or managing a firm. Plus, this is really a second income for my family.

I will call you next Wednesday to discuss a possible fit. I am anxious to explore any opporrunity to work with you on some exciting, creative, and high-profile projects.

Sincerely,

Tammy Shanahan

Michael David

1 Peyton Drive, Boston, MA 00000
(508) 555-5555

September 22, 20__

Jennifer Johnson
Michael-Graphics
909 Dallas Parkway
Dallas, TX 75240

Dear Ms. Johnson:

Lead. Follow. Or get out of the way. That modus operandi has been behind the drive that helped me achieve a nearly perfect GPA at the University of Texas (2003 graduate) and win the highest leadership honors in the College of Business there. As the top ad agency in north Texas, Michael-Graphics is my first choice for an internship this summer. I have worked very hard and succeeded at the highest levels in college, and I am hungry to work (even as an intern) at the top firm as a natural progression in my career.

I have very strong software skills and recognize the need for research as a means to winning accounts and uncovering successful strategy. As you keep your firm on top in a very competitive environment, new account acquisition is critical to growth. Product, industry, and firm research can open many doors to new opportunities. I recognize this and even enjoy it as a means to the end.

My extracurricular activities include summer employment in the Marketing Research department at Nokia and assisting the University of Texas/Austin with launching a new after-hours learning program.

I have worked hard to achieve academic success, and that is the best leading indicator I can provide that I would be an asset to your team. Thanks for your consideration. I will call you Tuesday morning to discuss this in more detail. Have a great day!

Sincerely,

Michael David

John Marano
jmar@usafinance.net
214 555 0000

Jaime Cantu
Principal, Castle Hills Elementary
Dallas, Texas

Dear Mr. Cantu:

I understand you are seeking a teacher for the new middle school opening in the Dallas ISD in the fall of 2009. I am very interested in this opportunity and excited about the prospect of teaching there. I am formally applying later this week, but I really wanted to drop you a quick note of introduction. I graduated from the University of Texas in 2003 with certification in elementary education.

Since then I have worked for two years as a teacher at Subley Middle School, and I was able to introduce a variety of teaching methods that included experimental games and cooperative learning activities. These encouraged a free exchange of ideas among students and produced measurable improvements in classroom participation and knowledge retention.

I grew up in Plano and am pleased at the possibility of returning to my hometown area.

I am sending you via FedEx my resume, a copy of my application, letters of reference from my current principal and two peer teachers, and a list of references from my students' parents.

Thanks in advance for any consideration. I am really looking forward to speaking with you about this in more detail.

John Marano

BARBARA O'TOOLE
1 Madison Way, Irvine, CA 91111 949.555.1111
bot@qway.net

May 29, 20__

Ms. Kathy North
Senior Director, IT Systems
999 John Carpenter Freeway
Las Colinas, TX 72222

Dear Ms. North:

I understand IT Systems is seeking a programming and UNIX server technician. Attached is my resume, demonstrating very strong experience in UNIX programming and network development; I carefully reviewed the specific requirements of the position, and it is a very close fit with my experience, as the front end of my resume, which highlights my credentials and accomplishments, will show you.

As a member of the IT development team for Nokia for the past six years, I was instrumental in creating advanced computer systems that cross industry boundaries. My prior experience includes an exemplary military career, where I was involved in planning and managing highly complex communication projects to support worldwide operations. My other work experience includes:

- Strong UNIX/Linux resource with Java and Tomcat experience.
- Strong network (WAN/LAN) knowledge, with good understanding of how relational databases work (MS SQL, MySQL, Oracle, etc.).
- Strong understanding of storage/backup basics (i.e., RAID, LUNS, SAN, remote network backups vs. local backups).
- Leader of IT department for Fortune 100 company and understanding of how "Big Company IT" works.

Ms. North, I traditionally own the technical relationship with one of our premier customers. I ensure that all technical issues are carried through to resolution and work closely with our Technical Account Management and Change Management teams to ensure that all aspects of the customer's ongoing system administration are successful. I am also available for escalations for my assigned customer 24x7 on a rotating, on-call basis.

I really do believe there is a potential fit based on what I read you are seeking, and I will call you next Monday to discuss it in more detail and set up a meeting. Thanks, and have a great weekend!

Sincerely,

Barbara O'Toole

Alice Scarpitti

3 Dallas Way
Grapevine, TX 75555
(972) 555-5555

Re: Student Counselor, Castle Hills High School—I'm a certified counselor with excellent references!

September 24, 20__

Mr. Roger Walker
430 Houston Way
Houston, TX 78444

Dear Mr. Walker:

I am so fortunate to be in the occupation I love—advising students. Although I do not have extensive experience in this field, the experience I do have has only furthered my commitment. As an advisor at Irving Central, I have begun to develop a coaching style that incorporates a thorough, flexible approach to accommodate the students' gifts and interests and maximize their probability of success. I am also devoted to continuing my own education. My true passion resides in helping students transition to adulthood, whether it be through continuing education or as they enter the workforce.

One reason I have chosen to apply for a position at Castle Hills is that it is rated so highly in the Houston area, where so many students opt not to go to college. If, after reviewing my resume, you believe there might be a match, please call me.

Mr. Walker, I have accomplished much as a professional in the private sector and now want to give back to the community, to pay it forward.

Sincerely,

Alice Scarpitti

11
Utilizing the Consultative Sales Approach

My day job is managing a sales organization for a Fortune 100 company in the telecommunications industry. Several years ago, we began to employ a new selling strategy called *consultative sales* to penetrate what we call enterprise accounts, the Ford Motor Companies and Exxons of the country. Prior to this new sales strategy, our sales teams would call on these accounts and preach the good word about our services with limited connection to how our services would *enable* them to do better things.

Since we put this new strategy into practice, our share of wallet (the percent of the total business available that we are awarded), jumped over 40 percent in 18 months, a huge success when you factor in the competitive environment in price and services and the long cycle in enterprise sales.

This made me think . . . if we apply these same principles to penetrating a company where we want to work, it would have to be successful. We should approach potential employers not just touting how great we as candidates are, but how we understand what their needs, objectives, and goals are and how our contribution will *enable* them to get there.

Marketers attempt to create and position a product to meet the needs of their target sales segment. You, too, should position yourself in a manner that meets the needs of your targeted employers. Once the marketing people do their thing, it is up to sales to complete the process. This is the place, or distribution element of the marketing mix. Your sales element is in full force when you are in the interviewing stage, but even prior to that you need to set up the stage for a strong sell.

In some industries, sales is nothing more than transactional, meaning that the sales department is selling a commodity type of product, simply taking and filling orders. A company that provides long-distance service to businesses is a good example. They are selling a simple product that has many alternate vendors, and the product may have few differentiators other than price. The salesperson doesn't have to sell a concept or stress the relationship between the customer needs and their product, other than the ability to make calls for less.

However, what if the salesperson worked for IBM's consultative branch touting Real Solutions? Then they would sell an integrated solution that might include long distance along with managed network services, Internet access, data transport products, and WAN service. In order to make that sale, the salesperson would absolutely have to understand the needs of the customer.

Enter consultative sales. Consultative sales calls for you to really understand the needs of the customer (or your prospective employer) and tell them that you have a product to meet those needs. So in order to rise above the pack in the job search process, you need to demonstrate to the prospective employer that you clearly understand their needs and you can fill the gap they have in their organization to meet those needs.

Here are a few examples of things to look for in an organization. These are things you should understand and research prior to beginning the cover letter process, so that you can address those items in your communications. Research:

- Their existing products
- Their new products
- Their geographic presence
- The climate of their industry
- Competitive products and companies
- Emerging trends both in their industry and within their organization
- The profile of current staff
- The profile of desired staff skill set
- Their key business or market drivers

There are many others, but you get the point. You need to try hard to learn about these things. Then you can better position yourself as someone who can help them achieve their goals rather than someone who needs a job. The research should take place prior to sending the cover letter and resume, so you can then customize them to meet the needs you uncovered.

You can learn about these things in several ways. The Web is a great place to start to learn about the industry or the organization. You can order their annual report or call various employees and ask them about the organization in the context of the bullet points listed here.

When you have uncovered that information, you can use it in two ways. In your resume you should position, spin, or highlight your accomplishments consistent with their overall goals. Your cover letter is the vehicle to formally address what you have learned and how you can help them meet their goals.

Take a look at the next few letters and examine the ways each letter opens with a level set of where the company is and where it is going. Then notice the way the writers are connecting the company needs with their own skills. If you can master this concept, you will be very successful not just in your job search but in your overall career.

Aidan Owens
I Castle Way, Fort Worth, TX 77777 817.555.1111

_____

January 12, 20___

Patti Coury
Clearwire Communications
1 Main Street
Irving, TX 77777

Dear Ms. Coury:

After completing much research on the wireless communications industry over the last few months, it has become apparent that Clearwire holds a unique position in the market. Clearwire has secured multiple WIMAX licenses across the country and, when built out, will have a national presence comparable to AT&T and Sprint.

In order to meet your aggressive growth goals of launching this market by next fall, you will certainly need a strong RF team that has experience in the CDMA platform. Specifically, you will need a team that has experience optimizing the Lucent and Nortel base stations.

As a consultant, I led RF teams from network design to launch with Verizon Wireless and Sprint PCS in the Chicago and Dallas MTAs, both of which were on a Lucent platform. I can provide excellent references from both. I think Clearwire is a cutting-edge operation, one in which ingenuity, creativity, and drive can make a material impression. I want to be a part of your team.

My experience is in perfect line with your needs right now and what you will need after launch. I will give you a call next week to set up some time for us to talk further.

Sincerely,

Aidan Owens

Kate Angie

111 Thompson Street,
New York, NY 00000
dg@renrd.com

November 29, 20__

Ms. Jamie Dergewrt
Principal, CCF Ltd.
1 Baltimore Way
Baltimore, MD 00000

Dear Ms. Dergewrt:

Your controller, Mr. Andy Wright, told me over golf a few weeks ago that you are looking for an MIS director. He told me some very interesting things about CCF and I was impressed, not only with the growth and profitability but with the similarities between CCF and Diversified Centers, my current employer. CCF has added 23 new training centers in the U.S., as well as overseeing the design of all Jack Nicklaus courses. With that much widespread activity, MIS needs must surely be exploding.

Given CCF's national profile, you must need each site to be networked with your home office for both voice and data transport, as well as establishing a WAN to improve real-time connectivity. As well, the design aspect of the business must eat up a lot of bandwidth in data transport, so it would surely help if you could share information more quickly and efficiently, while maintaining your privacy firewall.

My current operation is quite similar. Diversified Centers builds and manages strip mall shopping centers for Tom Thumb grocery stores. I have built a very efficient network for communications among our many regional locations. Our network enables each regional office to stay in touch via e-mail and shared drives through our WAN, as well as utilize the Sprint ION network for real-time communications of high-bandwidth development plans, similar to your use of golf course designs.

It appears that my accomplishments with Diversified Centers is in line with your MIS needs at CCF. I will give you a call next week to set up a meeting to talk further.

Looking forward to meeting you,

Kate Angie

P.S. Andy told me you are acquainted with Mr. Nicklaus. Please congratulate him on his fine Masters showing!

Michael Gusola

1 Strickman Lane, Houston, TX 77777   mg@ret.com   682.555.1111

December 2, 20__

Mr. Jamie Smith
Touchstone Creative
1000 O'Connor
Las Colinas, TX 77777

Dear Ms. Smith:

Jim Talley, at Touchstone, recently informed me that you are overseeing costumes and makeup for the new film *The Nutty Professor*. Jim mentioned some of the effects that you are planning to use to transform the lead character from the thin professor to the very overweight professor. In order to pull this off, you will undoubtedly need artists skilled in this field.

The plastics, makeup, special wraps, and various maskings take a great deal of skill to apply in a way that is undetectable to the viewer. I know; I was the lead artist for several movies and clips, including Michael Jackson's *Thriller* video, *Halloween H20*, and several *Tales from the Crypt* episodes.

My experience is very consistent with what you will need for your upcoming film. Please review my attached resume for the specifics of my film credits. You will see that my skills are a good fit for helping you with the makeup and related preparations for the demanding transformation scenes. I will call you next Tuesday and set up a time to stop by the studio to meet you.

Sincerely,

Michael Gusola

Tracie Gusola

1 Baybrook Avenue, Friendswood, TX 77777, (682) 555-0000

June 9, 20__

Ms. Dina Eschler
Administrator, Trinity Medical
1 Josey Lane
Carrollton, TX 75056

Dear Ms. Eschler:

Over the last few months I've noticed your firm moving into consulting with several health-care firms. After speaking with Ken Elder, I am aware that you are bidding on the upcoming opening of two new HCA hospitals. You will no doubt need significant health-care industry expertise to drive this account. Health-care clients can be complex to handle when you are trying to balance aggressive marketing and sales techniques with a hospital's image as a public entity.

The openings of the two new locations in Portsmouth and Springfield will require delicacy, given the amount of bad press HCA has received in the last year or two. HCA has been in trouble with both the IRS and the FBI for tampering with federal aid and overbilling Medicare. They will undoubtedly need good advice on how to position their openings to get off on the right foot.

I have been working in marketing and public relations for nine years, most recently with Humana in Florida. We successfully opened eleven new hospitals over the last six years, and even experienced a storm when we opened the one in Orlando. That hospital opened in the midst of a major citywide controversy regarding the for-profit nature of Humana versus the general reputation hospitals have maintained for operating for the good of the people. Under my direction, Humana successfully overcame that hurdle, and now that hospital is one of the most successful in the region.

My skills are very much in line with the needs of both your firm and your clients:

- Fifteen years in public relations
- Fifteen years in the health-care industry
- Expertise in new launches and crisis management
- Key contacts within the industry

Please expect my telephone call in the next week so that we might be able to set a time to meet and discuss employment possibilities that would serve our mutual interests.

Sincerely,

Tracie Gusola

To: Jeff Luedcke
From: James Trolly
Date: March 1, 20__
Subject: Network Engineer Position

I have been researching AT&T and their place in the integrated services offerings for some time. I was intrigued to read about the upcoming INC announcement that is currently scheduled for this fall. INC is reportedly going to converge data and voice transport products into a single, more cost-effective transport that can support virtually unlimited bandwidth demands.

In order to pull this off, you will surely need to have strong relationships in place with the CLECs or ILECs in given markets. In the short run, that is the only way you can provide the local access "last mile."

I have considerable experience working with Bell Atlantic/Nynex and Bell South in xDSL. xDSL will surely be your plan for last-mile access when it is built out, and you will need skilled network data engineers to optimize and design that integration.

Please take a look at my resume, which reflects the broad experience I have acquired in data transport and xDSL technology. I will call you next week for an appointment, at which time we can review this further.

Sincerely,

James

To: Dave Ryan

From: Dean Grant

Date: February 15, 20__

Subject: Call Center Operations

Congratulations on the recent contract between the pilot's union and management. The strike of 1997 was surely devastating, not only to UPS, but to the nation as a whole, which depends on and trusts UPS. The agreement signed last week ensures that the good name of, and extraordinary service provided by, UPS will not be tarnished.

I read in the business section of the *Chicago Times*, over a month ago, that UPS was expanding its call center operations in the Chicago area and that a benchmarking effort was going to be made to bring the center back in-house after many years of subcontracting the service. Now that the talk of strike has been put to rest, I am sure you will again be focusing attention on this project. I believe I can help!

I work as a call center manager for Sears, Roebuck and Company here in Chicago. They, too, once contracted out their call center/customer service operation and made the decision to bring it in-house six years ago. I was one of nine team leaders responsible for the strategic planning and implementation of the conversion from contracted to in-house call center operations for Sears. I was part of this team from the very beginning to now. Over that six-year period, we improved our customer service rating from 93.7% to 99.2% while saving the company approximately $1.2 million. I implemented a tactical plan to further enhance the rating to 99.7%, and now I am seeking new challenges.

Some of my career highlights include the following, which actually tie in closely with the emerging needs at UPS:

- Personnel management and team building; directing a team to consistently exceed organizational expectations
- Systems and operational benchmarking; developing systems of operations that can be replicated in other operations
- A highly competitive but congenial management style that inspires success while demanding results
- Strong finance/budget management skills; bottom line oriented

I am sure that you see the connection between my areas of strength as stated above and the criteria by which UPS evaluates potential managers. I know your time is extremely valuable, and so is mine. Therefore, I would enjoy speaking with you for a few moments over the telephone to determine whether an in-person meeting might be beneficial to us both. Please expect my call next Monday afternoon. If this is not a good time to chat for a few minutes, we can arrange another time that is mutually convenient.

Thank you for your time and consideration.

Sincerely,

Dean Grant

To: Charlie Stevenson

From: Hank Yule

Date: April 13, 20__

Subject: Retail Leadership

Darren Washington let the cat out of the bag! I think it is in the best long-term interests of our industry that Horrace Small Manufacturing enter the retail segment of the law enforcement uniform industry and compete with the other manufacturers who have begun to travel this road. There is no doubt, you will assume a leadership role in the retail operations as you have in the manufacturing arena. And I believe I can contribute to this success.

I have enjoyed working with you and your company over the past nine years as a vendor and retail client. We have certainly shared some great success stories. When I first began Professional Image Uniform Company in 2000, few people gave me a chance to succeed, but Horrace Small (Darren Washington in particular), the giant of the uniform industry, saw my potential and accepted me as a retail customer. Today, nine years later, Professional Image Uniform Company is one of the largest uniform companies in the nation. We even bought out Simons Uniforms, a company that tried to thwart our success. I am proud of what we accomplished and feel no regrets about selling the company to FSS, Inc., because I am now seeking a new and more exciting challenge.

Might that challenge be to spearhead your national retail operations?

Darren mentioned that you are presently looking for a retail manager to direct operations at your flagship location. I am interested in meeting with you to discuss this exciting opportunity. I have one more week to finish up things with FSS and then I am available to meet in Nashville. I will call you tomorrow to discuss this.

I have six areas of accomplishment that truly do connect closely with the needs of Horrace:

1.   An industry-recognized track record for successful retail start-up management from conception to implementation
2.   Multiple retail operations management
3.   Creative sales, marketing, and promotions tactics to accelerate growth
4.   Inventory management expertise to ensure five-star customer service with minimal inventory levels
5.   Competitive positioning—understanding competitive influences and developing tactical strategies to be number one
6.   Organizational/personnel leadership; hiring attitudes and inspiring peak performance

Charlie, thanks for taking the time to review this note. I'd really love to get together for a few minutes soon to talk a little more. There is no doubt in my mind that we'd make a great team in pursuit of your retail growth objectives.

Sincerely yours,

Hank Yule

To: Misti DeOrnalles

From: Frank Julian

Date: December 19, 20___

Subject: Sales Contribution

Our paths have crossed on at least two occasions, and I was truly impressed each time. Please allow me to explain. I attended the Executive Women's Association gala event three weeks ago at the Cypress Creek Marriott, where more than 400 people assembled. When I drove my car to the valet, I was awestruck by the professionalism of the attendants, the uniforms, and the courtesies extended, not only to me, but to everyone. I mean to say that the valet service was so exceptional, it was the talk of the evening!

When I asked to speak to the hotel manager to rave about the valet service, he told me that it had nothing to do with the Marriott. I found out that your company is responsible for this level of service. Last Saturday night my husband and I went to the Kravis Center to see *Phantom of the Opera*. Needless to say, half of South Florida was there—and so were you! Again, I could not believe the level of service provided.– It was simply exceptional.

So our paths have crossed on two occasions over the past four or five weeks, and I'd like to propose a third meeting. I am a highly successful sales professional and I will only represent companies with top-rated products and services. I would like to propose a meeting to discuss how I can best help your company grow and prosper even beyond the success you have had to this point.

After completing some research online, I discovered your Web site. I noticed that your company has plans to expand into Broward County as well as Martin. I know I can use my plethora of corporate contacts to help you build your company. And if you decide you want to go regional, state, or national, I have the experience and verifiable track record to assist in this area as well.

And here's the best part: I enjoy being compensated for results, and I guarantee results. I do not require a high base salary compensation plan, but actually prefer an attractive commission program. I am a six-figure earner and am compensated only when I bring in the business. My past sales experience has been focused on hospitality-oriented business, so I have key contacts with companies that can use professional valet services. In fact, I have spent the last three evenings studying the valet business and have familiarized myself with the competition, past and future trends, and growth/profit potential. Based on my preliminary findings, you are in a niche market with almost unlimited potential.

I have enclosed a detailed resume of my qualifications and will contact you early next week to discuss possible scenarios for future employment with your company.

Thanks for taking the time to read this letter. I do hope we can meet in the next week or so.

Sincerely,

Frank Julian

Kevin Rounder
21 Village Street San Francisco, CA 99465 kr@oer.com
(302) 555-0000

February 2, 20__

Ms. Alice Greene
Center Plaza Hallmark
201 Broadway, Center Plaza
San Francisco, CA 99427

Dear Ms. Greene:

Bonnie Taylor provided me with your name and suggested I contact you regarding summer employment this season. Apparently, Bonnie has worked for you for the past three summers but will be in Europe this year and thought I might work in her place.

I understand you are looking for people who have experience in retail environments, are customer service oriented, are loyal and dependable, have working knowledge of point-of-sales computer technologies, and are drug free. It can be so difficult to find good people in retail environments like this. The retail stores I have worked with at school have really struggled to get good, bright, and courteous people on staff.

I am in my third year at UCLA, majoring in business administration. As well, I have five years of retail experience (The Body Shop, Wolfe Camera, and The Gap) and am very familiar with POS computer systems.

I will be off for the summer as of May 29. However, I will be home for spring break (April 7–15) and would like to stop by and introduce myself to you. We can both be sure that Bonnie would not have introduced us to each other if she didn't feel I could fill her shoes in a way that measures up to your high standards.

I will call you next week to see if we can arrange an interview during my spring break. Thanks in advance for your consideration.

Sincerely,

Kevin Rounder

Kathy North
3232 West Collings Avenue, Windsor Heights, IA 50311   (508) 555-0000

March 2, 20__

Mrs. Shirley Snife, Chairperson
Windsor Heights Girls Softball League
99 Town Center Road, Dept. A-6
Windsor Heights, IA 50398

Dear Shirley:

It is no secret that Windsor Heights has developed a woman's softball program that is the talk of the state. I read in the local newspaper a week ago that there are more than 160 women participating in the league and that the emphasis on skills training is so intense that Windsor Heights has won the State All-Star Championship in each of the past two years. It is a credit to you and your staff that you have met an important need in our community—namely, providing our children with the resources and opportunity to compete in an area that they love.

I also read in that same article that you are looking for volunteers to coach these girls—that there are four or five openings for coaching and assistant coaching positions. I have a fifteen-year-old daughter who has played in the league for the last two years. Having been an active parent, I think I have a good idea as to what you are looking for in a coach. I offer you the following:

1.   More than eleven years' coaching experience as an assistant athletic director at the high school level
2.   The ability to grasp and teach the fundamentals of the game
3.   The ability to inspire players in a positive way, to give 100%, and to achieve peak-performance levels
4.   A teaching approach that emphasizes sportsmanship
5.   The ability to work with parents, league staff, and others involved in making this program a success

I know that there are limited head coaching positions available, and I would very much welcome the opportunity to assist a head coach in hopes of demonstrating my abilities for a future coaching position.

I will be attending the board meeting scheduled for March 24, and I hope to meet with you before then to properly introduce myself to you. If you would like to speak/meet with me prior to the meeting, I will make myself available at your convenience.

I look forward to another great season and hope to become a participating member of your coaching staff.

Sincerely,

Kathy North

To: Ernie Holland

From: Michael Waterson

Date: March 9, 20__

Subject: Client Executive Program

Dear Mr. Holland:

I understand you are seeking to add a client executive to the Chase financial family in the north Texas area. From the research I have done, Chase is ranked fourth-highest financial institution in total assets both nationwide and in Texas.

However, the commercial lending business in Texas is ninth. To grow that business, you will be looking for someone who:

- ☐ Understands the commercial sales business
- ☐ Can lead a strategic sales planning session, develop a plan, and execute it
- ☐ Can hire and retain the best B2B sales individuals
- ☐ Is a strong leader and closer

For the past five years I have led the commercial sales effort with Citigroup in Texas in two vertical segments and in those market segments. When we began the channel five years ago, our market share was eighth, and we have grown it to second. We did this by making personnel changes in our team, and then implementing a strategic selling process.

My specific strengths include:

- Assessing sales talent
- Interfacing with C-level decision makers
- Developing selling strategy based on the needs of the customer

I will call you early next week to discuss your needs further. Thanks, and have a great weekend.

Sincerely,

Michael Waterson

S. Dave Ryan

1 Germantown Lane, Baltimore, MD 00000

December 7, 20___

Grant Guillen
Division President, Leap Communications
200 Mission Bay
San Diego, CA 99999

Dear Mr. Guillen:

Leap Communications has achieved tremendous market penetration over the past year. The new market launches in Texas, Florida, and California have completely changed the wireless landscape. The big three carriers are forced to react to the changes you have brought about in the market, and the customer is the benefactor.

I read in an FCC filing that you plan to launch the Baltimore-Washington market in the third quarter of next year. In preparation for that, you'll be establishing your sales channels by the first quarter. Based on what I've seen in other markets, you will be launching a small direct retail channel, a very robust indirect channel of local and national retailers, and a small B2B effort.

I have worked for a first-tier wireless provider for over ten years, in multiple capacities. I launched a direct retail channel, from site selection to initial staffing and training. Our first-year productivity per store was in the top five of fifty-three markets nationwide. After managing that channel for about eighteen months, I moved to run our indirect channel.

Our indirect channel in the Baltimore-Washington area established over 800 points of presence. My team of indirect sales managers and account executives recruited these agents (about 20% were nationals) and supported them via training and materials. This channel became number one in the nation, even toppling former number ones in south Texas and TDMoS. I am certain I can replicate this success and shorten the launch curve as Cricket enters the market.

My interest in Cricket is the tremendous value play the market desires. I will call you next week to set up a meeting.

Sincerely,

S. Dave Ryan

Dan Schmitz

1 Plaza Space
Kansas City, KS 00000
(816) 555-0000

August 12, 20__

Mr. George Taylor
Phillips HC
1 Metcalf Place
Overland Park, KS 00000

Dear Mr. Taylor:

The biotechnology and pharmaceuticals industry has struggled over the past couple years. The industry's 336 public companies took in revenue of $55.5 billion, a 14 percent increase.

* The aggregate net loss of those public companies was $3.5 billion, a 151 percent increase over the net loss of $1.4 billion in 2005.
* Market capitalization fell 3.9 percent to $392.4 billion.
* Twenty initial public offerings raised $944 million, compared with the $626 million raised by thirteen companies in 2005.
* U.S. biotech companies signed drug development deals worth as much as $23 billion, an all-time high.

In this challenging time, the need for astute professionals in the industry is heightened. I am a management professional attuned to the ever-changing needs of business. My success lies in my track record of identifying market plan needs, creating actionable programs, and effectively interacting with the sales field. I am extremely service oriented, with a unique combination of intuitive and analytical abilities:

- Robust analytical and problem-solving skills

- Methodical, investigative, and creative

- Specialized in the physicochemical and mechanical characterization of solids

- Knowledgeable about formulation science, physical pharmacy, and analytical chemistry

- Well acquainted with most of the instruments and techniques used today such as UV, FT-IR, HPLC, DSC/TGA, powder X-ray diffractometry, scanning electron microscopy, light microscopy, VTI water sorption analyzer, GMP dissolution, BET surface analyzer, and helium pycnometer, among others

- Experienced in solid dosage form design and development

I am certain there is much I can bring to PHC—at a minimum, the possibility is worth exploring. Please expect my call next Tuesday and perhaps we may set up a time to talk.

Sincerely,

Dan Schmitz

To: Lisa Cee

From: Derek Fielder

Date: January 27, 20__

Subject: South Florida Ritz-Carlton

Ms. Cee, I understand from Thomas Delton that you are not pleased with the performance of your marquee property. Some specific challenges Thomas pointed out include:

- Human resources issues

- Technology

- Customer issues

- Operating cost creep

- Airlines in the twenty-first century

Clearly, the fact you are below the company averages in occupancy and corporate events identifies an opportunity at the property level. I have always held Ritz-Carlton in high esteem as an elite brand and offering. I would love the opportunity to be a catalyst in bringing your property to a high performance ranking within the organization.

Here are some career highlights as evidence that I can deliver on the promise to grow this property:

- Consistent track record of successfully turning around faltering operations and creating profitability and excellence; utilize keen assessment and problem-solving abilities, dynamic training techniques, and key motivational strategies that build accountability and enhance staff performance.
- Responsible for the small group corporate, sports, and universities channel markets for the Ritz-Carlton, Atlanta, and the Ritz-Carlton, Buckhead. Accountable for approximately $1.3 million in guest-room revenues in 2004 and exceeded first-quarter goal by 10 percent.
- Maintained aggressive solicitation process to increase new business in the local Atlanta market. Assisted in the preparation of annual forecast, marketing plan, and conversion to Delphi. Forecast group room nights and rates for all definite business within territory.
- Specialized in sports and small corporate meeting negotiations. Built and established relationships through ongoing entertainment, sales calls, site visits, and trade shows.
- Graduate of several of Europe's premier hotel management/culinary institutions; professional management experience through employment with some of Europe's most prestigious establishments and a Boston four-diamond hotel; fluency in English, German, and French.

Lisa, I am very interested in speaking with you. Please call me at you earliest opportunity.

Best regards,

Derek Fielder
404-555-0000

Michael David
101 Bobby Way • Detroit, MI 48221 • md123@httryw.com

February 8, 20__

John Anders
Delphia Company
1 Birmingham Street
Birmingham, MI 48207

Dear Mr. Anders:

Delphia has a great selection of products and is the leading supplier to the auto manufacturers in Detroit. However, based on what I am hearing from within the industry, there are some human resources challenges in existence. I have spent the past seven years working for Ford Motor Company, and we are close enough to our largest partner for me to see some opportunities. From what an outside source tells me, there are varying levels of opportunity in the following areas:

- Employee turnover costs
- Inconsistent employee hiring practices
- Employee absenteeism
- Poor customer service
- Poor employee motivation
- Poor team development
- Productivity improvement

We have faced theses challenges at my company, too, and I'd welcome the opportunity to share our practice improvements. I am a strong HR generalist with proven talent in the development and implementation of training programs for exempt and nonexempt personnel, as well as proven ability to develop material, impart knowledge, and update programs as needed.

- Strong research and analytical abilities; notable experience in the management and reduction of costs related to liability and insurance.
- Recruiting activities included all aspects of screening, interviewing, hiring, and orientation for union and nonunion staff.
- Continuously updated knowledge relevant to workers' compensation, ADA, EEO, Family Medical Leave Act, OSHA, DOT, etc.; developed and implemented new procedures to ensure compliance.
- Benefits administration experience includes program development, maintenance of costs through negotiations, and development/implementation of alternative benefit programs.
- Implemented training and development initiatives that have been proven to improve retention and morale.
- Generated ongoing bottom-line savings through the introduction of various cost-cutting programs.

Please expect my call Friday to discuss any help I might be able to offer.

Sincerely,

Michael David

Barry Halverson
3 Dragon Way, West Palm Beach, FL 33409

March 27, 20__

Justin Jacobs
Roddick Group
101 Central Expressway
Dallas, TX 75555

Dear Mr. Jacobs:

Advertising that is suspected of being false, misleading, or deceptive may be challenged under the auspices of one or more of the regulatory authorities. Advertising challenges may originate from three broad areas: government regulation, industry self-regulation, and third-party lawsuit.

Advertising challenges can derail marketing plans and result in onerous penalties. Furthermore, today's advertising challenges are as likely to originate from a competitor as from a government agency. Regulatory authorities are increasingly being employed as a competitive marketing weapon.

Based on what I have seen from the Sunbelt mishap, there is some opportunity at Roddick. Please forgive me in advance for appearing forward, but Teresa Strasser suggested I contact you. I really do care about driving an advertising campaign aggressively but in the right way. My career represents a dynamic and proven twelve years' marketing and advertising experience with demonstrated success in agency, consulting, and Fortune 1000 environments.

- Acumen for developing solutions using the full complement of the marketing and promotional mix, inclusive of database, PR, sales promotion, events, and online channels.
- Ability to organize complex variables and build partnerships, then orchestrate internal and external resources toward shared objectives while maintaining clear communication and positive relationships. Put into practice self-initiative, attention to detail, and a standard of excellence.
- Reputation for completing projects on time and within budget with solutions focused on meeting marketing and promotional metrics, articulating strategic communications objectives, and maximizing production efficiencies.
- Polished interpersonal and communications skills, with public speaking and presentation abilities. Wide range of computer systems and software knowledge and experience.
- Ability to manage an advertising operations support team of eight with a sales budget of $58 million.

I would really like to sit down with you and explore any mutual opportunities. My client and in-house references are very strong, should that be of any interest to you. Please expect my call late Monday afternoon.

Sincerely,

Barry Halverson

Marcos Cancel

111 Thompson Street,
New York, NY 00000
mc@renrd.com

April 25, 20___

Mr. Steve Zeine
United Assistance for Children
1 Baltimore Way
Baltimore, MD 00000

Dear Mr. Zeine:

Your counselor, Valerie Buffet, mentioned to me that you are looking for some assistance in your fund-raising effort.

She shared with me some of the wonderful work you have done to assist and develop children in need in the metro area. Obviously, the fuel to support those efforts is fund-raising, mostly from the private sector. The ability to coordinate events, tap into the wealthy donors, and create awareness for the UAC is critical to your growth and long-standing existence.

I have spent the latter years of my career in this business. At this point for me, giving back is the most important endeavor in which I could engage. A senior manager with a Fortune 50 company for much of my career, I am somewhat connected with many potential donors, and I possess an understanding of the process. I have been involved in philanthropic activities for the past five years. Below are some highlights:

- Started, organized, and managed nonprofit campaigns for four years.
- Executive director experience at both local and national levels.
- Responsible for the formation and incorporation of an all-volunteer 501(c)3 charitable organization, including corporate charter, articles of incorporation, IRS status request generation, and internal procedure definitions. Successfully completed state, federal, and local registration for an organization with gross income over $100,000 by the second year. Successfully negotiated rent-free associations with pet supply businesses for pet adoption locations.
- Raised over $4.2 million in the past five years.
- Five-year consistent record of attaining projected fund-raising targets.
- Reduced volunteer turnover of 38% to less than 8% annually. Increased donations 123%.

I'd love to help, if you see a fit. Feel free to call on me anytime.

Sincerely,

Marcos Cancel

GREG FANTIN

1 Melbourne Way, Denver, CO 33333 303.555.1111
pm@west.net

July 23, 20__

Mr. Brian Majesty
Vice President, Kijo Corporation
1 Pikes Peak, CO Springs, CO 00000

Dear Mr. Majesty:

I understand Kijo is seeking a general manager to lead the Colorado operations for the new chemical-related sales operation you are launching. In order to successfully accomplish this, the GM candidate needs to lead his team to meet with customers and suppliers and work with the scientists on product offers. This group provides the link between the technical staff at a company and its markets. Whereas scientists always interact with customers on specific product issues, sales and marketing managers track the long-term needs of a market and focus research on these needs.

Generally, sales marketing managers are assigned a product line and a territory. They spend a good deal of time traveling and meeting with customers in their territory. They also attend between six and ten trade shows each year, where they make contacts with customers and representatives from other companies. Most of the chemical sales personnel have degrees in chemistry (BS, MS, or PhD) and generally use their chemical training daily.

My background closely fits this profile. I have a BS in chemical engineering and have spent my career in sales, working my way up in this industry. My time has been spent with the top two industry leaders (reflected on my resume), and I have demonstrated progressive career growth with these two Fortune 100 companies.

Now I would like to take my experience to a smaller but up-and-coming firm. I will contact you early next week to set up a meeting.

Sincerely,

Greg Fantin

Leigh Ann Epperson

1 Charlotte Way
Norman, NC 11111
704.555.5555

February 7, 20__

Mr. Colton Claye
Quality Assurance
1 Main Street, Suite A
Charlotte, NC 55555

Dear Mr. Claye:

Caden Halverson, a customer of yours for the past several years, mentioned that you had a growth rate of 8% and might be looking for someone with diversified experience. Caden and I each coach a little league team and have been associates for the past two or three years. When he mentioned your company, I was very impressed by his praise for the originality of your work.

I have decided to offer my services to a company like yours that is faring okay but looking to realize greater growth than what you have had. In the past decade, I have acquired experience in three fields that, I think, are of interest to you: administration, production, and sales.

- **Administration**: I worked on security designs for many different organizations, including commercial complexes, apartment and residential properties, and several schools.

- **Production**: I coordinated the efforts of four implementation teams that have worked on many different installations and services.

- **Sales:** Our operation has grown steadily each of the past four years, realizing over 30% growth a year, and doubling it twice year over year.

I am most interested in the opportunity to meet with you and discuss how I might make a positive contribution to your company. I will call you next week to see when you have time for a meeting.

Sincerely,

Leigh Ann Epperson

12

Letters for Students

Crafting a cover letter as a student is not materially different from creating other cover letters. The examples that follow will give you some idea of how to phrase your academic accomplishments, internships, and your postgraduation desires.

You will find that different companies will recruit at different universities, trying to be geographically diverse, focusing on the top schools only, or focusing on those schools that have brought them the best recruiting success in the past. Resumes from these targeted schools will often be reviewed with a little more attention than resumes sent through the mail or by fax. There are a few exceptions, however.

If the company you are targeting doesn't recruit at your school, you still have good options, and you may have to employ the tactics discussed later in this chapter. If your targeted company is visiting your campus to recruit, you should register with the school's career center to obtain an interview. When that is scheduled, do some preliminary research on that company. Most on-campus recruiting companies are large enough to have a detailed Web site and be "in the news." Visit their site so you can see their direction, and conduct some media searches to learn more. Then, drop this information into the interview where appropriate. You will learn more and make a stronger impression on the interviewer.

Now suppose your targeted company is visiting your campus, but you cannot secure an interview because of your major or grades. Don't give up; employ some creative tactics.

- Try having a favorite professor "sponsor" your effort, and try to either work with the campus career center or the recruiter to grant you an interview.
- Make a special effort with the dean of your department or the director in charge of the career center to convince them that you are worthy and should not be overlooked. If your grades are poor, it may help to have some justification, such as working 20 or more hours per week. If you have a different major, point out that over two-thirds of all professionals work in fields that are different from their emphasis in college.

Suppose the company is large, like Verizon. Go to a Verizon store and network with the store manager to see whether someone internal can get you any additional pull to secure an interview. There are many ways to get in the door, and you should not give up at the first push back. Also, if the company is recruiting, perhaps you can get an interview even if you do not get one on campus. If you know that a bigger, nationally known company is recruiting, go directly to them and apply for a position.

If you have secured your interview on campus, perform some research on the company so you are prepared to discuss how you can fit into their organization. Your research should stimulate good questions to ask the recruiter. In addition, here are some sample questions to consider, posed as if you were interviewing with Verizon:

- What brought you to Verizon and how does it differ there from other places?
- How would you rate the overall leadership and direction at Verizon, and how is overall morale?
- How would you describe the management culture at Verizon?
- What is one characteristic that demonstrates leadership skills in your organization?
- What do you feel is your biggest competitive threat in the next several years?
- How would you describe the culture of your company?
- Could you describe a typical day in the life of a [whatever discipline you're interviewing for] person?
- What are some of the challenges you face on a day-to-day basis?
- What is the average length of time entry-level recruits remain with Verizon?
- Did your company face significant layoffs in the most recent recession, and if so how were those who were laid off selected?
- What types of continuing education programs do you offer your employees?
- What support mechanisms are currently in place that foster your company's innovative culture?

LEVERAGE FACULTY AND ALUMNI

College grads and seniors should use their college's alumni for networking sources. Generally speaking, most people are pretty willing to help you network if you ask them to do something specific or provide general advice. The trick is getting in the door to those connected professionals. Here are some tips on networking with alumni.

- If you hear of alumni presenting at your college, go there, make sure you make contact with the presenters, and ask for their business cards for future reference.
- Ask professors in your discipline if they know of any graduates who work in the area you are interested in or for companies you are targeting.
- Suppose you are interested in obtaining an accounting job with Ford Motor Company. Go to other professors, such as those in the engineering department or marketing department, who might be connected with alumni or managers at Ford. Keep in mind that large companies employ people in a wide variety of disciplines, and you should leverage any "in" you can uncover.
- Find out which faculty members work in the consulting arena in the private sector and seek their advice and contacts.
- Focus on recent graduates/alumni. They were more recently in your shoes and may be better sources of tips/leads than more established alumni. Go to alumni gatherings, such as football games at sports bars and the like. To put this tip in perspective, in Dallas, the Michigan State University alumni association has over 100 members. Alumni, especially from major universities, are *everywhere*.
- Make sure you treat alumni as respected networking sources and utilize the principle outlined later in this section. Don't send them your resume, and don't ask them for a job. Be well organized and think through what you want to ask them so they can give you targeted advice. If you are not focused, they will not be able to help and may find the whole exercise frustrating.

CAREER FAIRS

Career fairs are a much overlooked venue for uncovering good career opportunities. Grace Matherly, 26, was looking for a new marketing job in Dallas. She networked with some former colleagues, checked the classified ads, and contacted some executive recruiters. Still, she had not yet uncovered the position that was the best fit. Then she heard of a career fair for engineers and technical managers. Though she was not looking for that type of position, she went anyway, to network.

There she met some recruiters from Sprint, and found out that the company had a big marketing presence in Dallas and that they were hiring. Sixty days later, armed with that information, Grace secured exactly the position for which she was looking. She uncovered an opportunity that had not been advertised and had no executive recruiter supporting it.

Even if the career fair is for a specialty other than your own, it still provides an excellent networking opportunity to uncover new leads. Generally, career fairs are advertised in local papers and held at hotels or convention centers, and from 5 to 15 companies may be participating—even more at large fairs in major markets.

Career fairs can sometimes be crowded, with long lines of candidates waiting to interview. You can maximize your productive time with good preparation. Try to register electronically at the organizer's Web site if possible. This eliminates standing in line at the entrance. Get there early, before the long lines, if you can. No matter what time you show up, go first to the companies that your research has indicated will be the best match—and then hit the rest. Do take the time to visit as many companies as you can. Following are some tips to ensure that you get noticed.

- Develop your "elevator pitch." This is a two-minute overview of your background and the type of position for which you are looking. It should include professional/academic information, not personal information. However, when delivering it, you can interject some personal information to build rapport, demonstrate a high-energy personality, and distinguish yourself. Just don't overdo it.

- Bring at least one good copy of your resume for each company participating in the fair, as well as a few extras in case you network in other areas.

- Research the employers attending. This point cannot be stressed enough. Learn more about the company, its product/services, and current challenges. You can find terrific information on their Web site and in media reviews. Some of this information can be garnered from going to the company's trading symbol on financial Web sites and looking in the "news" sections. Also, you can simply type in the name of the company in a good search engine and click on what comes up.

- Bring a folder to carry resumes and a notepad for notes.

- Dress professionally. Dress professionally. Dress professionally.

- Prepare for the interviews. Consider picking up *Great Answers, Great Questions* (McGraw-Hill, 2004) as well. Prepare questions you want employers to answer.

- Go alone; if you go with friends or family, walk the fair by yourself.

- Be aware of time demands on employers. Do not monopolize an employer's time. Ask specific questions and offer to follow up after the fair, as appropriate.

- Be direct. Introduce yourself. If you are job seeking, state the type of position in which you are interested. If you are gathering information, let employers know that you are only interested in materials and information.

- When greeting a recruiter, introduce yourself and look confident by initiating a handshake with a smile.

- Ask the company what the next step is and how to follow up.

- Get appropriate contact information and ask for a business card.

- After the career fair, send a thank-you card and reconfirm interest in the position and company. In the note, say exactly when *you* will follow up, and then do so. Put the burden of follow-up on yourself because, although the company may intend to, chances are they're too busy and will put it off or forget.

Roberta Alexander
111 Wylie Street, Danachestnut, TN 00000

November 15, 20__

Ms. Elise Ford
Director of Marketing, United Chemicals
101 Dallas Street, Suite 600
Nashville, TN 00000

Dear Ms. Ford:

I will be graduating from the University of Tennessee this spring with a degree in microelectronics engineering. I thoroughly enjoy the sciences and selected this discipline because it is the most challenging the university offers.

I have ranked in the top five in my class within this discipline, inarguably one of the most difficult U-T offers. For the past year I have had my eye on the possibility of joining United Chemicals when I graduate.

What are the qualities you deem most important in a candidate for a position with United? As a college graduate, I have not had wide paid experience. However, I do bring fresh talent to be shaped professionally, a strong academic record to indicate future success, and a hunger to join the workforce.

- The curriculum for the BSE program emphasizes design and strong computer experience. The program is designed to provide a sound foundation in mathematics, basic sciences, engineering science and design, communications, humanities, and social sciences, with an emphasis in the option area (mechanical design or manufacturing) in the senior year.

- I joined Dominion as an intern this past summer, and worked side-by-side with their professionals, learning new skills and sampling new technologies involved in the energy industry.

- During the previous summer, I interned at George Washington College and attended a series of seminars to learn how government officials make decisions on complex technological issues and how engineers can contribute to legislative and regulatory public policy decisions.

My objective is to secure an entry-level position with United Chemicals upon graduation. I am particularly interested in the use of radiation in medicine for treatment, a new area for United.

I have enclosed my resume along with a letter of recommendation from the chair of my department at U-T. I look forward to speaking with you soon. Please expect my call next week.

Sincerely,

Roberta Alexander

Lance Paulley
3 Dragon Way, West Palm Beach, FL 33409

January 12, 20__

Angela Armstrong
Trinity Technologies
Boynton Beach, FL 33333

Dear Ms. Armstrong:

The summer prior to my graduating year took me to my first internship, in the sales organization for Hewlett-Packard in San Jose, California.

I learned so much supporting the sales staff there and have decided it is my chosen discipline. I enjoyed the prospecting, the presenting, and the research that go into connecting the product offering to the company needs. These are skills I would like to put to work for Trinity Technologies.

One area I really took to was the strategic selling aspect of the process. I enjoyed the research on company needs, where the opportunities were, and how the HP offering can help these companies get to where *their* strategic goals were.

While at HP I was on the team that presented and eventually sold to Cisco Systems and Sun Microsystems.

I will receive my BA in marketing in May of this year. I will call you later this month, and please look for a contact letter or reference from Michael Jerald at HP.

Sincerely,

Lance Paulley

Greg Fantin
I Castle Way, Fort Worth, TX 77777 817.555.1111

January 12, 20__

Jim Finn
Wentworth Engineering
Irving, TX 77777

Dear Mr. Finn:

Grace Fruit suggested I contact you to express my interest in joining Wentworth when I graduate this spring from the University of Texas/Austin with a BS in electrical engineering.

Last summer I interned with Hormel Foods, which was a wonderful experience. I was involved in plant electrical distribution, electrical coordination studies, industrial controls, access control, time and attendance, electrical safety, and power measurement software. I updated engineering information, conducted system testing, evaluated results, and made improvement recommendations following these assignments.

It truly reaffirmed my commitment and interest in this discipline. My attached resume also lists several of the key projects I worked on at school, including the next revolution in copper-based broadband access to provide order-of-magnitude improvement in DSL access speed and quality through innovations in both physical-layer and network architecture.

Additionally, I have worked as a team leader for Habitat for Humanity in Austin. There I learned leadership skills and how to coach for performance, putting the right people in the right areas for maximum utilization of skills.

I will contact you next week to discuss this in more detail. Thanks in advance for your consideration.

Sincerely,

Greg Fantin

KELLI WILLIAMS
1 CHICAGO WAY, CHICAGO, IL 00000

March 29, 20__

Ms. Christine Zach
Sprint Communications Company
2001 Michigan Avenue
Chicago, IL 00000

Dear Ms. Zach:

From what I have researched, penetrating the WiFi marketplace and being second to market in a soon-to-be-commodotized industry mean that the marketing work done at launch must be done right the first time or it will be difficult to recover in the future.

I can help you launch this new service offering right the first time. I am a recent graduate with an MBA in corporate communications and broad sales, marketing, and public relations experience in the telecommunications industry. Since completing my undergraduate studies, I have worked for T-Mobile Communications, learning the WiFi strategies relative to their Hotspot service offering.

Since then, I have watched the industry closely and feel that Sprint is positioned well, owning the widest breadth of spectrum. Still, it will hurt not being first to market.

My education and practical experience in the industry, and the fact that I am interested in joining at a grade 76–77 level, should make me a terrific candidate for consideration.

I will call you late next week to set up a meeting. Please see my resume, attached.

Looking forward to speaking with you soon!

Sincerely,

Kelli Williams

Samuel Jacinto
1 Quarry Way   Stoneham, MA 00000   (508) 555-1111

July 16, 20___

Ms. Lori Harding
Senior Partner
Robert Half and Associates
1 Harbor Town
Boston, MA 00000

Dear Ms. Harding:

Thanks for speaking with me today. The public relations and marketing disciplines are certainly my passion, and the prospect of joining this national firm in a very competitive environment is exciting!

My resume is enclosed. You mentioned that the new candidate should be familiar with the recruiting industry, which is my schooled discipline. I interned for four months last year with Snelling and Snelling in Dallas, and, while I did not wish to work there postgraduation, I learned a great deal about the industry.

During my internship, I worked on client projects in the areas of expert recruiting, niche industry research, and other strategic initiatives. I was assigned my own projects and managed these projects from conception to completion during the course of the internship. Tasks included the following:

- o   Closely assisted top executive recruiter in daily initiatives.
- o   Recruited highly intelligent industry leaders and academics.
- o   Effectively marketed a unique proprietary business model in the fastest-growing segment of the independent research business.

Ms. Harding, considering my education, my industry internship, and my communication strengths, I am confident that this position would be a wonderful mutual fit.

Thanks in advance for your consideration. I will give you a call on Friday to discuss this in more detail.

Sincerely,

Samuel Jacinto

To: Dylan Roberts

From: Manny Tamble

Date: June 12, 20__

Subject: Corporate Communications Manager

Mr. Roberts, please allow me to introduce myself. My name is Manny Tamble, and I am following up on your advertisement for a corporate communications assistant. I believe you will find my background and skills to be an excellent match.

I am graduating from Michigan State University in the fall of this year. While there, I placed in the top quarter of my class. More important, to prepare myself for the next step postgraduation, I worked the past three years within my discipline.

I worked at NPR and conducted research for daily stories and long-term projects, booked interviews, retrieved archival tape, attended daily editorial meetings, and helped get programs on the air, which included performing routine administrative tasks. In addition, I assisted the public and media relations department in the planning, execution, and publicity of events.

I believe my academic and part-time employment background make me an excellent candidate for the corporate communications manager position.

Thanks! I look forward to speaking with you soon.

Manny Tamble

PATRICIA HENDRICKS   Beach Road One, Miami, Florida 33333 ■ (954) 555-0000

July 1, 20__

Dr. Bridgid Nesbit
1 Castle Way, Suite 400
Castle Hills, TX 75556

Dear Dr. Nesbit:

Dr. David Ryan mentioned to me that you were seeking a dental assistant as you expand your office. I have been taking classes at Dallas Community College and am obtaining my certification from their dental technician program.

My schooling has prepared me for the following activities of a dental assistant:

- Preparing patient for treatment.
- Selecting and handing instruments to the dentist during dental procedures.
- Sterilizing and disinfecting instruments.
- Setting up instrument trays.
- Suctioning the patient's mouth.
- Applying fluoride coating to teeth.
- Pouring, trimming, and polishing study casts.
- Examining orthodontic appliances.
- Exposing dental diagnostic X-rays.

I would appreciate the opportunity to talk with you in greater detail. I will call you next Monday to answer any questions you may have, and possibly to secure a meeting.

I look forward to seeing you.

Sincerely,

Patricia Hendricks

Grace Fruit

1 Caroline Way ▪ Newark, NJ 75555 ▪ gf@tt.org

___

March 4, 20__

Mr. Michael Jackson
American Tradition Group
14 Park Avenue
New York, NY 11111

Dear Mr. Jackson:

I am responding to your advertisement for an entry-level insurance adjuster at American Tradition Group.

I am a recent graduate of Rutgers with a degree in business management and a minor in mathematics. I have always enjoyed math, but chose a business degree for my primary focus, to increase my marketability.

Success in the claims adjustment discipline requires the ability to investigate, analyze, and determine the extent of the insurance company's liability concerning personal, casualty, or property loss or damages, and an attempt to effect settlement with claimants. The adjuster also needs to be able to correspond with or interview medical specialists, agents, witnesses, and claimants to compile information, and then calculate benefit payments and approve payment of claims within a certain monetary limit.

Based on my academic experience, the inherent capabilities required by the field that I possess, and my passion for the business, there really is a good mutual fit here. Please contact me to arrange for an interview.

Best regards,

Grace Fruit

Omar Omari

1 State Street   Houston, TX 77777   (281) 555-1212   oo@mmm.com

February 26, 20__

Patrick Rail
Friendswood ISD
Baybrook, TX 77777

Dear Mr. Rail:

I am formally applying to become the physical education teacher at the Baybrook Middle School for next year. As a recent graduate with a degree in physical education, I am eager to enter the professional workforce and begin applying my passion for teaching. Enclosed is my resume.

As an approach to teaching in general, one can adopt an authoritative delivery or a more patient approach to ensure understanding. Having been a student much of my life, I have always valued the latter approach and am committed to that style of teaching and leading.

During my last two years in college at Texas State, where I achieved a 3.35 GPA, I also worked as a personal trainer at a local 24 Hour Fitness.

Sandy Duckworth, a science teacher at your school, mentioned the opening in the physical education department. She has known me for several years, and I would be happy to have you speak with her about me. Sandy mentioned an opening for the coming school year and suggested that I contact you. I would love to set up a meeting in the next couple weeks to discuss the opportunity.

Feel free to contact me anytime, and if I do not hear from you, I will call you the week of March 10.

Thanks, Mr. Rail!

Omar Omari

Leslie Perry
101 Round Rock Way, Round Rock, TX 75555 lp@erc.org

August 12, 20___

Ms. Tia Sanders
Sea World and Busch Gardens Entertainment
1 Addison Drive
San Antonio, TX 75240

Dear Ms. Sanders:

I am interested in applying for the Sea World summer internship position that was listed through the University of Texas bulletin.

I have had a great deal of laboratory experience in chemistry and marine biology, as well as personal experience, having logged over 100 dives in the field. In the lab, I have performed many biological experiments on marine life diet, and I am currently using microscopes to observe many specimens. In environmental field studies, I have conducted outdoor labs to assess water chemistry. This truly is my passion, and I would just about pay you for the opportunity to work on the grounds at Sea World.

Last summer, I worked at Six Flags Over Texas, providing experience in the theme park line of work. I am seeking to complement my academic experience with a research internship in order to acquire the background necessary for a future career in marine biology.

I am certain that I would be an asset to your program. This internship would provide me with the ideal opportunity to assist at your organization and to expand my research skills.

I will call next week to see if you agree that my qualifications are a match for the position. If so, I hope to schedule an interview at a mutually convenient time. I look forward to speaking with you.

Thank you for your consideration.

Sincerely,

Leslie Perry

To: Paul Quail

From: Mark Stroonge

Date: June 3, 20__

Subject: Financial Analyst Position

I would like to express my interest in an entry-level analyst position with Beckman Fields. Through my job search and conversations with investment advisors, I have come to respect the reputation that the company enjoys as an industry leader.

I am confident that I would highly complement the Beckman group's values and objectives with my own strengths and enthusiasm. I would like to be considered for your financial analyst program, or for a similar position that requires refined analytical and communication skills.

I was impressed to learn of your firm's recent acquisition of JJW, a move which I see as indicative of Beckman's commitment to achieving growth and success in the future. Innovative and exciting initiatives such as this, coupled with your highly regarded financial analyst program, convinced me that Beckman Fields would be an ideal environment as I launch my business career.

Evidence of my leadership and analytical skills can be seen in my responsibilities as analyst intern at KKR and my commitment to academics. At Northwestern University I achieved a 3.4 GPA, with a major in economics. My graduation is set for the end of this summer.

Please review the enclosed resume and references and consider my application for your financial analyst program. I would appreciate the opportunity to come to New York to meet with you to gain an understanding of your firm's objectives and culture. I will call you next week to see if we can set up a time in the next two or three weeks.

Thank you for your consideration, Mr. Quail.

Mark Stroonge

ELIZABETH WEBSTER

1 Madison Way, Irvine, CA 91111 949.555.1111
cd@qway.net

March 31, 20__

Dr. Robert Porter
Chairman, School of Lindsey
999 John Carpenter Freeway
Las Colinas, TX 72222

Dear Dr. Porter:

I am writing in reply to the classified ad seeking to fill the position of undergraduate student advisor for the graduate business administrator program.

I have obtained my master of arts degree in accounting and business administration from Michigan State University, and I understand the need for academic advisement and program planning for undergraduates as they map their course toward graduate work. I have also experienced firsthand the positive effect of being able to contact an advisor who genuinely cares about the success of students.

During my graduate studies, I held volunteer office hours to counsel and support undergraduates in their studies and ensure they met the requirements for pursuing graduate work, should that be their objective.

This volunteer work really helped me find my passion and calling. This is exactly what I want to do upon graduation.

I believe my educational background and my work in counseling and advising students have prepared me well for the official role as student advisor. I am able to provide several references from professors in the college of business at Michigan State as well as from students I advised and with whom I worked. I will call you next Tuesday to set up some time for us to talk in more detail about this opportunity.

Sincerely,

Elizabeth Webster

Dean Rappa

1 PR Way, Puerto Rico 00000
(487) 555-5555

April 2, 20__

Michelle Bristow
Director of International Science
Smithsonian Institute
Washington, DC 00000

Re: Guide Director of Natural History

Dear Ms. Bristow:

I have formally applied for the position of guide director for the Museum of Natural History, but I wanted to drop you a quick note. While studying history at Georgetown University, I spent much of my time pursuing the arts as a personal passion.

I am seeking to put my skills to practical use, combining my education and interest in the arts to work with the most respected organization in the country. Although the guide director position caught my eye, I am open to other positions within the organization.

I worked for a summer at the Museum of Natural History in New York and during high school I interned and volunteered at the Metropolitan Museum of Art as well. Within my history major, I took four courses on art and would be equally interested in that branch of the Smithsonian family.

I am excited at the prospect of evolving from being a patron of the arts to being a part of this field professionally. I will call you next Monday to see whether there is a possibility of us meeting face-to-face and to discuss this and any other opportunities that would represent a mutually beneficial fit.

Best regards,

Dean Rappa

Wes Scott

1 Brady Drive, Boston, MA 00000
(508) 555-5555

March 20, 20__

Maureen Hannah
Presbyterian North
909 Dallas Parkway
Dallas, TX 75240

Dear Ms. Hannah:

Thanks for speaking with me today. I am interested in beginning my professional nursing career, ideally in prenatal care or pediatrics, two areas in which you said there would be openings this year.

While I know you have my resume, I would like to highlight some skills and accomplishments that make me an ideal candidate:

- o   Recent graduate from the Harris School of Nursing, placing in the top quarter of my class.
- o   Served in assistant, noncertified capacity for Ready Texas Nurses, the Web-based emergency response system of Texas that's intended to provide an effective response from nursing in times of crisis and disaster. We responded to the devastating disaster created by Hurricanes Katrina and Wilma.
- o   Schooled in the specialized areas of:
    - o   capillary blood glucose monitoring and collecting venous blood specimens by venipuncture (practice on mannequins)
    - o   Intravenous therapy infusion pumps and patient-controlled analgesia, and central venous catheters
    - o   Gastric decompression
    - o   Enteral feedings
    - o   Suctioning, tracheostomy care, and ostomy care

Ms. Hannah, Presbyterian North is where I wish to work, and I am certain this represents a mutual fit for your organization and me. Please feel free to check the references I have provided, and I will be back in touch at the end of the week.

Have a great week!

Wes Scott

Dawn "Lucy" McCarter

101 Longhorn Way, Dallas, TX 75240   972 555 0000   dawnillmccarter@ill.com

June 22, 20__

Michael M. Master
Master, Woods, and Buda
4 Spartan Drive
East Lansing, MI 48888

Dear Mr. Master:

Justice Timothy Brown, of the Lansing Court, mentioned to me that you will have an opening soon for a legal assistant. Judge Brown has known me and my family for many years, and mentored me while I pursued my education to become a legal assistant and paralegal.

I will be graduating this summer from the University of Texas, though I now regret not going to Michigan State, because of my desire to work in that location. Still, UT has been a wonderful experience for me. I will receive a BA in English; however, I also studied business administration and accounting and am highly computer literate.

No one knows exactly how legal services will be handled in the next several years. As paralegals, we may be able to play a greater number of roles than either lawyers or secretaries. Regardless of the type of legal environment we work in, our professionalism and expertise in the way we perform legal services will either enhance or detract from the reputation of the practice we support, both within the legal profession and with the public. Not many professions offer the opportunity to make such an important difference, and I take that very seriously.

I am excited to be embarking on this profession. Feel free to contact Judge Brown or the references from my legal work in Austin that appear on my resume.

I will call you next Thursday to discuss the opportunity further. I will be in Michigan for a few days beginning on August 17, so perhaps we can meet then.

Sincerely,

Dawn "Lucy" McCarter

To: Trey Humphries

From: Seth Miller

Date: May 23, 20__

Subject: Entry-level nuclear engineering position

Dear Mr. Humphries:

The other day my mother asked me why I chose nuclear engineering as my college major, and my answer surprised me as well as her: "Because it is the hardest."

Given that answer, it's not so surprising that my first choice for a company with which to begin my career would be Atomic Power. In the world of power generation, it is the biggest and the most diverse, and, I'm hoping, presents the greatest challenge.

What are the qualities you deem most important in a candidate for a position with Atomic Power? Although as a recent college graduate, I have not had wide paid experience, I believe I can offer the necessary fundamentals to be an effective contributor to the Atomic team.

   • As an intern, I performed work of above-average complexity that conformed to all project/task requirements, including defined scope, schedule, and budget, and that required an independent understanding and application of engineering theories, complex calculations, and computer codes for design applications, standards, concepts, and techniques as well as knowledge of engineering industry codes and government regulations.

   • I am able to provide technical support for daily operations, plant improvements, process improvements, design, equipment acquisition, plant breakdown and analysis, self-assessment, technical procedure reviews, corrective actions, root cause analysis, critical path analysis, and detailed review of vendor engineering products.

   • I have a BS in industrial and mechanical engineering.

My current goal is an entry-level nuclear engineering position with Atomic Power for early this summer. I am especially interested in nuclear fuel reclamation and waste disposal. I have enclosed my resume along with an official Atomic Power application. I hope what you see there will encourage you to consider me as a candidate. Thank you for your attention, and I very much look forward to hearing from you.

Sincerely,

Seth Miller

DORIS FRONTLY

1 Von Karmon, Irvine, CA 99999
df@qqqr.com

March 14, 20__

Ms. Kristin North
Director of Operations, HCA
999 John Carpenter Freeway
Las Colinas, TX 72222

Dear Kristin:

Your associate, Dr. Glenna Thomas, advised me that he has sent you my resume so that you might consider me as a participant in Trinity Health Care's Clinical Laboratory Science internship program. I have enclosed another copy of my resume for your convenience. Please contact me if I can provide you with other documentation that will help with your decision making.

On June 3 I will graduate from the University of North Texas with a bachelor of science degree in clinical laboratory science. I am currently completing my third year in the honors program curriculum at UNT, and am confident my education has prepared me well for a senior internship.

Dr. Thomas and others have spoken highly of HCA's training program. It is precisely the type of challenge I seek. In return, I offer a solid foundation of relevant knowledge. Unlike other applicants who may have a more general background, mine includes four years of combined experience in medical research and health-care settings. My background would allow me to be a highly productive member of your clinical program.

The opportunity to work with your program would be a real asset as I start my career, and I would appreciate your serious consideration of my qualifications. Thank you for your time, and I look forward to hearing from you.

Sincerely,

Doris Frontly

To: Misti DeOrnalles

From: Frank Julian

Date: December 19, 20__

Subject: Sales Contribution

Ms. DeOrnalles, please allow me to introduce myself:

I am responding to your advertisement for a corporate communications assistant, and I believe you will find my background and skills to be an excellent match.

Believe it or not, I worked my way into my current position as writer/editorial assistant for a prestigious newspaper publication company from the bottom up. I started out as the mascot, dressed in yellow tights and wrapped up in a newspaper—definitely not the most dignified position I've ever held, but it does show that I'm willing to do whatever the job requires.

Having recently obtained my BA in corporate communications to round out my skills and knowledge, I would like to find a position in a corporate setting where my strong communication skills could be of value. As you will see on the enclosed resume, I have developed many comparable abilities through my long-term employment with the California Press.

As an enthusiastic communications professional, I believe my background and skills can fill your need for a corporate communications assistant. Although I would prefer to avoid the mascot gig again, I would certainly be eager to discuss any related communications or PR positions that would match my abilities.

Thank you, and I look forward to hearing from you soon. I promise you won't be disappointed!

Sincerely,

Frank Julian

Grace Matherly

1 Moon Drive, Houston, TX 77777 832.555.1111 gm@tygle.net

September 5, 20__

Elsie Coxon
Recruiter (contract)
Western Alliance Corporation
1 Okeechobee, West Palm Beach, FL 33409

Dear Ms. Coxon:

Your client has the opportunity to enter a new, potentially lucrative resort market in the Southeast, nobody knows his corporate name, and aggressive rivals are breathing down his neck—that's his nightmare.

His dream? He is at the helm of a highly competitive market leader, a resort destination considered first in its field, with a reputation for customer service, innovation, and making dreams come true. His is the first name that springs to mind.

I can do that for him.

I am a recent graduate with an MBA in corporate communications and broad sales, marketing, and public relations experience in mature, high-growth, and transitioning resorts. I can point to outstanding marketing and PR communication successes during this last decade with the renowned Sunset Bald Inn; my graduate studies have honed my skills in developing internal as well as external corporate communication strategies.

Have you a client in need of my skills? I am open to relocation anywhere in the Southeast.

I look forward to further conversation.

Best regards,

Grace Matherly

To: Jeff Kilpatrick

From: Mark Ludwig

Date: April 11, 20___

Subject: General Marketing Manager Position

Dear Mr. Kilpatrick, please allow me to introduce myself:

I have always believed the three keys to successful marketing are product knowledge, product support, and perseverance, but the greatest of these is perseverance.

Let me explain. First of all, it is important to know your product inside and out, in order to sell the benefits. Second, it is extremely vital, especially within highly technical markets, to provide ongoing support. And last, but certainly not least, it is the company with the most persistent sales representatives (armed with the first two keys) that will ultimately clinch the sale.

During my tenure with Conn's Electronics, I have had the opportunity to develop my professional skills in many areas and I have learned how to succeed in a highly competitive and ever-changing market. Starting as an account executive, I have worked my way into the position of sales manager. I am proud to say that my sales figures, both individually and as an area, have consistently increased every year. I truly believe that half of this success has been due to the product knowledge and support information that I have been able to convey, but the other half was definitely due to my undying persistence.

Having recently obtained my MBA in marketing, I am now ready to take my career to a new level as a senior manager in marketing, and I would appreciate the opportunity to meet with you at your earliest convenience. If you require additional information, please feel free to contact me.

Thank you for your time and consideration. I look forward to hearing from you soon.

Sincerely,

Mark Ludwig
214-555-0000

Michael Gerard

3 Dallas Way
Grapevine, TX 75555
(972) 555-5555

January 8, 20__

Ms. Tammy Cancela
430 Houston Way
Houston, TX 78444

Dear Ms. Cancela:

Learning can be a fun and rewarding experience for both adolescent and facilitator, which is why I am responding to your ad for a part-time teacher assistant that appeared in the July issue of the Castle Hills newsletter. I will be graduating from UNT with a bachelor's degree in education. I have actively remained on the dean's list for the past two years and my cumulative GPA is 3.2.

Your opening stands out from those I've entertained from other schools due to the unique way art and music are incorporated into the learning process. This position offers the opportunity I desire, integrating my formal music training with my interest in developing children.

You will find that I am capable of meeting your qualifications:

- **Team Player:** I understand that my role is to support the teaching staff in daily operations including materials and meal distribution, arrivals and departures, toileting, and other related functions.

- **Creative Activities:** I am formally trained in classical and folk guitar and would welcome staff collaboration on the best utilization of this talent. While at the ISD, I introduced a popular art project in which children made kaleidoscopes from household objects and materials.

- **Parent-Staff Relationships:** Having worked in the educational field for the past six years, I understand the importance of fostering a family-friendly environment where parents and staff work together in the best interests of the children. During my tenure at the Board of Education, I developed congenial relationships with parents and caregivers, alerting them to any unusual occurrences during the school day.

I welcome the opportunity to discuss program needs and will contact you early next week to schedule a convenient meeting time. Thank you for your consideration.

Sincerely,

Michael Gerard

13
Functional Areas of Expertise

Many clients have expressed interest in having letters and phrases that emphasize the need for functional areas and transferable skills, to complement the traditional letters based on the usual disciplines such as finance, accounting, or health care. This really is a good idea for two reasons:

1. Many of you will (or should) pursue opportunities outside of your industry.
2. These letters will stimulate how to take your functional accomplishments and translate those into words for prospective employers.

This chapter includes example letters from the following areas:

- Coaching
- Cost reduction
- Driving performance
- Employee satisfaction
- Initiative
- Managing conflict
- Negotiating
- Negotiating offers

- Organizational skills
- Presentations
- Problem solving
- Reengineering
- Time management
- Writing skills

Memo

Date: 9/16/20__

To: Catalina Valencia

From: Sheri Simasek

Re: Coaching Experiences

Catalina, as a follow-up to our meeting, you asked me to send you some details around my coaching accomplishments. Below are some of my key coaching-oriented highlights:

❖ Designed and implemented a seven-week management development program focusing on critical competencies that managers need in order to be effective: management/leadership roles, performance management, communication, coaching/motivating staff, Situational Leadership, decision making, delegation, and conflict management.

❖ Developed a 360-degree assessment program, including action plans and follow-up surveys for individual management development and increased effectiveness.

❖ Designed and piloted team development project to increase managers' understanding of team dynamics and team building, including stages of team development, dysfunctions of a team, ensuring accountability, team performance, organizational change, and facilitation skills, resulting in higher team performance.

❖ Facilitated, designed, and implemented intensive training lectures, seminars, and course curriculum; excellent career and personal coaching abilities.

❖ Taught classes on anger management, budgets and financial counseling, and diversity in the workplace, conflict resolution, crisis intervention, team building, and personal coaching techniques.

I will contact you next Wednesday to follow up on our meeting. Have a great week!

Sheri

Memo

Date: 4/4/20__

To: Penny Lane

From: Paul McKenzie

RE: Examples of Coaching Accomplishments

Penny, thanks so much for our meeting. I too believe the position we discussed is a strong mutual fit. Given the emphasis your firm places on people development, I would like to reiterate some of my accomplishments that I believe make this such a great opportunity for both me and the company:

❖ Conducted 360-degree feedback sessions for thirty-seven executives/managers to gain a better understanding of their strengths and development needs; assisted them in developing strategies to leverage their strengths within the organization and develop their management skills for increased effectiveness.

❖ Developed staff to meet and exceed company goals and objectives through coaching techniques, training, and corrective action. Assumed advocate role developing and writing training courses based on training deficiencies as outlined from specific work groups.

❖ Created and implemented "Coaches Corner Tips" to cross-pollinate sales/service scripting, improve product knowledge and soft skills, and increase sales techniques.

❖ Executive coaching and leadership development: partnering with various business directors/executives to coach and consult them regarding their business challenges, helping them to improve their performance and to achieve their business goals and objectives. Coached a founder/CEO regarding how his behaviors influence his organizational culture and environment.

❖ Advised, problem-solved, and coached management regarding various organizational issues—organizational processes, coaching/motivating staff, and dealing with problem behaviors.

I am very excited at the prospect of joining Pepperland Corporation. Please expect my call this Friday to discuss next steps.

Paul McKenzie

Kate Winters

1 Strongbert Way   Stoneham, MA 00000   (508) 555-1111

July 16, 20__

Ms. Stephanie Smith
Senior Partner
Robert Half and Associates
1 Harbor Town
Boston, MA 00000

Dear Ms. Smith:

Thank you for meeting with me Monday. I do believe there is a potential fit between your client and me. Below are some points you asked me to send you with respect to my experience and approach to cost reduction.

It's no coincidence that the most effective cost cutters are companies like Wal-Mart Stores Inc. and Dell Inc., which use technology to keep processes such as inventory management on the cutting edge. Cost reduction in general is a big part of business. It has always had its place, but more so since the economic climate softened in 2000. Events since then have complicated the issue of economic stability, and countless companies have taken drastic measures to reduce costs in order to remain viable.

While balancing the requirement to have a cost-effective marketing and distribution system with a progressive organization capable of generating explosive growth, the team I led identified cost containment and restructuring opportunities that resulted in a total 75-basis-point decrease in sales acquisition costs, a 32% reduction, while increasing sales to $2.3 billion, almost a 50% increase.

Cost reductions have allowed for additional promotional opportunities, increased price competitiveness, and a self-financed expansion into new distribution channels. Cost of goods sold reductions of 7.5% while improving customer-perceived quality of finished products affected our net income by over 3% year over year.

As well, we reduced direct labor costs by $12.5 million on an annual budget of $189 million and implemented employee incentive programs, cost-reducing operations by $1 million, which we believe increased both morale and productivity.

I look forward to discussing this in more detail next time we meet.

Sincerely,

Kate Winters

TANYA SELHOST

1 Madison Way, Irvine, CA 91111 949.555.1111
cd@qway.net

June 21, 20__

Ms. Jane Stoney
Senior Vice President, Cocoa Corporation
999 John Carpenter Freeway
Las Colinas, TX 72222

Dear Jane:

I am enclosing my resume and am very interested in pursuing the cost management opportunity for which you are recruiting. At my current employer, I accomplished the reduction of inventory by 24%, utilizing MRP (management resource planning), JIT (just-in-time Delivery), and value-managed partnerships with suppliers. As well, I directed a new corporate inventory reduction program, achieving a 15% reduction in inventories.

For the past eighteen months, I have been assigned as project manager for the PRI. In this role I am working with Global Shared Services to reduce total cost of ownership of digital output devices (printers, copiers, and faxes), establishing processes and standards, and enabling Web access and usage monitoring for cost containment and reduction of nonbusiness activities by minimizing unauthorized use. A 10 to 15% cost reduction was projected after a complete cost/benefit analysis and equipment inventory were completed.

This accomplishment made me a key member of an executive team responsible for the reduction of over $65 million in annual expenses prior to the purchase of Ameritech by SBC. There I introduced several procedural and methods changes, resulting in a 34% cost reduction on a specific product line.

I am certain this potential fit is worth exploring further. Please expect my call this Friday afternoon, and we can talk about it in more detail then.

Sincerely,

Tanya Selhost

David Watsky
3 Dragon Way, West Palm Beach, FL 33409

June 12, 20__

Jamie Smith
Global Support Organization
Boynton Beach, FL 33333

Dear Mr. Smith:

My organization led improvements in five key areas, resulting in a 53 percent increase in market value. My team's workforce management practices include:

- Implementing focused HR technology
- Opening up communications between management and employees
- Establishing a collegial, flexible workplace
- Creating a total rewards and accountability orientation
- Attaining excellence in recruitment and retention

Overcoming barriers to performance is how groups become teams. Managers and others often should pay more attention to helping team leaders perform. Assuming that the team approach really is the best option, the key to getting unstuck lies in addressing the particular obstacles confronting the team with a strong performance focus. There is no incremental performance expectation beyond that provided by individual executives working within their formal areas of responsibility.

These skills and accomplishments represent very transferable skills that can be directly applied to the People Resource Manager position you are creating. I am looking forward to speaking with you in more detail about this next week.

Sincerely,

David Watsky

Alex White
101 Waco Way, Waco TX 75555 tr@erc.org

July 2, 20__

Mr. Mike George
RTC Consumer Products, Inc.
1 Addison Drive
Addison, TX 75240

Dear Mr. George:

According to one of *Fortune* magazine's "Most Desirable Companies to Work For," hiring great people is the first requirement for high performance. One great person is equal to three good people, and one good person is equal to three average people.

The bottom line of performance is that organization success depends on how well the expectations of key stakeholders are met (customers, investors, employees, suppliers, and the public).

The ABC division, for which I worked, led performance at Goodwyn, a Fortune 75 company. Our operating redesign included the following issues:

- Benchmarking high-performance organizations and learning about high performance
- Assessing current organization strengths and weaknesses
- Creating an organization operating philosophy
- Designing the work system including jobs, roles, and responsibilities
- Designing a performance measurement and management plan
- Creating a capability-building plan: training and development experiences
- Developing a transition plan to manage the change
- Providing for continual renewal to ensure adaptation to a changing environment

I am excited about the prospect of bringing these practices to your firm. Please expect my call on Monday afternoon, and perhaps we can meet later in the week.

Sincerely,

Alex White

Denise Riley
I Castle Way, Fort Worth, TX 77777 817.555.1111

January 12, 20__

Michael Stone
Nokai Communications
Irving, TX 77777

Dear Mr. Stone:

Setting goals establishes a performance target for each activity, whether it is a daily sales goal, an annual one, or even the number of inquiries a call center processes. While general manager at PepsiCo, I set weekly targets of productivity for my team, and they responded by achieving a ranking in the top 4 of 130 districts nationally.

Further, driving high performance begins with leading by example. By leading the key activities for our success myself, my team learned both how to execute and that they needed to in order to be a true part of the team.

Our high-performance organization owes its success to its employees. We have great people, and have developed them and taught them how to achieve special results. This is an indication of a learning organization that provides training in the following areas: redesign of business processes, delegation of work, teamwork, companywide communication, shared vision, and advanced technology skills. A high-performance business improves faster than its competition and sustains that rate, while satisfying all its stakeholders.

Nokai is known for valuing high performance and, as such, I believe this represents a good potential fit for my skills and experience.

Sincerely,

Denise Riley

Tim Ralwey
1 Charlotte Way • Norman, NC 11111 • 704.555.5555

July 7, 20__

Mr. Jay Wasserman
Waltham Products
1 Main Street, Suite A
Charlotte, NC 55555

Dear Mr. Wasserman:

Based on our conversation yesterday, you indicated a need for improved employee satisfaction. High employee satisfaction is essential for the acquisition and retention of a quality workforce. Tracking the attitudes and opinions of employees can identify problem areas and solutions related to management and leadership, corporate policy, recruitment, benefits, diversity, training, and professional development.

Driven and motivated employees will be more creative and work harder to solve problems because they care about their career and about the company or organization for whom they work.

At P&T Enterprises, we increased productivity 25% overall with reduced staff turnover and high employee satisfaction by creating a positive teamwork environment, setting goals, and sharing the vision.

By consistently achieving high employee satisfaction, we minimized employee attrition numbers. After six months of our new program implementation, we maintained a 90% or better rate of retention for the senior seasonal staff team, and 0% turnover for full-time staff for two consecutive years.

I am excited at the prospect of bringing these programs to your organization. I'll call you next Monday to discuss this in more detail.

Sincerely,

Tim Ralwey

Jeff Kilpatrick

3 Dallas Way
Grapevine, TX 75555
(972) 555-5555

April 14, 20__

Ms. April Killen
430 Houston Way
Houston, TX 78444

Dear Ms. Killen:

Good managers and good companies realize that a happy employee is a productive employee. Poor managers might lead by intimidation or fear, or be too far the other way and appear lackadaisical. They can achieve results in the short run, but in the long run their employees will leave for a healthier culture. A good sports coach knows that to squeeze out that extra level of performance, the player must be motivated and driven.

I focused on building supportive employee relationships with demonstrated responsiveness and confidentiality. We also built a culture where we resolved employee/employer issues fairly and effectively, which contributed to high employee satisfaction.

In 2008 I was the recipient of the Award of Excellence at AT&T in recognition of exceptional employee relations for six consecutive years, as voted on by management. This award exemplifies the important characteristics of high integrity, loyalty, and dedication.

In addition to the specific accomplishments and experience my resume illustrates, you can see how important creating a culture of teamwork and high morale is to me.

I am looking forward to speaking with you soon.

Best regards,

Jeff Kilpatrick

George Starr

1 PR Way, Puerto Rico 00000
(487) 555-5555

November 19, 20__

Marie Holdonton
PeteTrade Financial
16111 Blue Ridge Circle
Palm Beach, FL 33440

Dear Ms. Holdonton:

The Southern Region flagship operation was one of the fastest growing and most profitable in the entire company. We also held the highest employee satisfaction rating of all the companies in the plastics sector. When we spoke last, you mentioned that was the most impressive accomplishment you saw under my responsibility.

In order to improve employee loyalty and satisfaction, we worked with management to create a program offering free, in-house leading industry certifications. This program offered employees optional classes in the evenings within our shop for courses leading to certifications such as MCSE and CNE. Visible improvements in employee satisfaction resulted, and we had less than 2% turnover during the program's two years.

During this time I was responsible for department and centerwide employee satisfaction results. We achieved improvement in employee satisfaction through implementation of employee-focused initiatives. I also organized and participated as a lead in task forces set up by management to improve employee satisfaction.

Employee growth was facilitated through a culture of openness, continuous feedback, and a practice of prompt decision making (most employee concerns were addressed within one working day). I am sure we can emulate what we did at SR at PeteTrade, given the chance.

I will call you this Friday to discuss this in more detail. Thanks in advance for your consideration.

George Starr

Aidan Riley

1 Brady Drive, Boston, MA 00000
(508) 555-5555

September 22, 20__

Christopher Silko
Silkography
909 Dallas Parkway
Dallas, TX 75240

Dear Mr. Silko:

In today's fast-moving business climate, success cannot wait for directives and long cycles for change to take effect. Executing strong initiative is critical to effecting change and making a difference with a sense of urgency.

As the leader of a portion of the sales organization, I managed and directed all facets of business development initiatives for the eastern region; I played an integral role in revamping sales philosophies and marketing strategies to successfully lead the division to the first profitable year in two years.

There we instituted a comprehensive, corporatewide performance metrics initiative with the slogan "You can't manage what you can't measure," resulting in proactive, instead of reactive, management of the company.

As a leader, team player, professional, fast learner, and detail-oriented, motivated, creative, adaptive, organized professional, I respect the need to work well with others, practice and promote diversity in the workplace, take initiative and be able to work without supervision, and perform with competence under pressure.

Qualities like initiative and that "sense of urgency" are characteristics one either has or does not have. I have a strong list of accomplishments and references to support my contention that I do, in fact, demonstrate initiative in all that I do. I look forward to discussing this with you when we meet this Thursday.

Sincerely,

Aidan Riley

To: Paul Pearson

From: Victor Jackling

Date: September 8, 20__

Subject: Strategic Sales Manager

Mr. Pearson, please accept this e-mail as a formal application for the SSM position for which you are recruiting. Attached is my resume, and I believe you will notice some very direct fits between your job requirements and my experiences and accomplishments.

Currently, my primary responsibility is for worldwide field engagement, specifically, aligning account managers with client business managers in AT&T's most strategic accounts.

There I developed and implemented a proactive teaming Initiative with sponsorship from both sales and marketing. This initiative required active facilitation of joint account planning meetings between the account managers and the client business managers to identify pockets of opportunity in those accounts. I was also responsible for developing additional incentive and promotional programs that lifted sales results 23% over the previous year.

I developed the proactive marketing initiative to maintain the company's leverage and protect future interests while meeting market expectations for standardization and integration.

Please notice the Fortune 500 "wins" we had under my direction.

I am looking forward to seeing you next week.

Paul Pearson

Debbie Davis
110 Cumberland Way, Atlanta, GA 30303

December 5, 20__

Justin Dawson
Director, Soft Drinks Inc.
1 Boca Way
Boca Raton, FL 33678

Dear Mr. Dawson:

As you mentioned the importance of seeing ideas through to a successful conclusion, I acted as liaison between executives, tenants, brokers, and corporation, managing conflict and ensuring shared understanding, as well as being accountable for coordination of final agreements.

My organization was responsible for driving change and managing a new staffing model utilizing "work-out" change by leading a team of 30 cross-functional managers.

- Facilitated several conflict resolution sessions between operations and functional groups.
- Facilitated new manager assimilation sessions.
- Facilitated change management work-out sessions.

Managing conflict successfully has more to do with acting as a coach than as a cop.

Please see my attached resume for specifics on my experience and accomplishments. As for the importance of conflict resolution, you can see that I value it as well.

I'm looking forward to seeing you next week.

Sincerely,

Debbie Davis

Maria Lane

1 Maryland Way, Baltimore, MD 00000
(301) 555-5555

January 29, 20___

Mr. Dave Ryan
Leap Technology
9911 Fairfield
Livonia, MI 48022

Dear Mr. Ryan:

My past successes demonstrate strengths in managing diverse job processes, building and maintaining relationships throughout an organization, motivating staff and colleagues, assessing and developing a high level of potential talent, and managing corporate objectives through major change.

I attended the following classes in the effort to hone my coaching and interpersonal management skills:

- ❑ Managing Conflict—AT&T School of Business, Course MS6431, completed July 2004
- ❑ Managing People and Performance—AT&T School of Business, Course MD7601, completed October 1993
- ❑ Certifications: Numerous technical and managerial courses: Managing Conflict, Managing People and Performance, Communications Workshop, Leadership for the Future, Achieving Communication Effectiveness, and Labor Relations (AT&T School of Business & Technology)

Conflict can be constructive, but if left to work itself out, the outcomes are seldom acceptable to all parties. Not only will mismanaged conflict disrupt the best of plans, it also dissipates energy and distracts you from your goals.

I will call you next Thursday to set up a meeting to discuss this in more detail.

Sincerely,

Maria Lane

Nika Niksirat

1 Charlotte Way
Norman, NC 11111
704.555.5555

February 7, 20__

Mr. Mike Cline
Quality Assurance
1 Main Street, Suite A
Charlotte, NC 55555

Dear Mr. Cline:

As you mentioned the importance of seeing ideas through to a successful conclusion, I acted as liaison between executives, tenants, brokers, and corporation, managing conflict and ensuring a shared understanding. I was accountable for coordination of final agreements.

In 2005 I was a contracted trainer for specialized workshop programs, leading programs in stress management, interpersonal communication skills, career management, customer service skills, conflict resolution, understanding and managing change, "Who Moved My Cheese?," team building, and assertiveness/self-esteem.

As a project leader managing several department contributions, I resolved conflicts between departments, conducted team leader meetings, and resolved all customer problems.

In 2006 I was selected local facilitator for the nationwide training broadcasts "Coaching Skills for Managers," "Planning and Organizing," "Oral Communications and Listening Skills," "Training Aids," and "Training Technology Update." I am a certified facilitator for group feedback sessions for managerial and support staff who completed the Performance Development System's training assessment instrument.

I developed and led conflict resolution programs in schools linking leadership programs with life skills awareness within a Baldrige in Education framework.

I certainly value the importance of conflict resolution and am excited about the prospect of bringing this function to your organization.

Sincerely,

Nika Niksirat

Thomas Delta
I Castle Way, Fort Worth, TX 77777 817.555.1111

March 31, 20__

Darrel Taylor
Karas Consulting
Irving, TX 77777

Dear Mr. Taylor:

Negotiation skills are an important part of business and life. You negotiate every day without even knowing it. The strength of your agreements, understandings, and relationships can mean the difference between success and failure.

Weak agreements with companies and individuals always break down. They bring nagging dissatisfaction and aggravation into your business and personal lives. Strong agreements help you reach and exceed your own objectives, and allow the other party to gain more satisfaction at the same time.

Negotiating is important for everyone, but particularly for those who work in sales, purchasing, or legal departments, or for any senior-level manager. While at GMC, I led negotiations for both enterprise and nonenterprise agreements with major software and consulting services suppliers that resulted in substantial cost savings, cost avoidance, and risk mitigation. With limited available negotiation leverage, we renegotiated software support agreements that resulted in dramatic decreases in total costs of ownership for software support and maintenance agreements.

Darrel, I am certain I can bring a significant improvement to your organization's contract negotiations for the upcoming partner agreements.

Sincerely,

Thomas Delta

To: Alicia Paramo

From: Beth Pasterz

Date: September 17, 20__

Subject: Key Negotiating Accomplishments

Alicia, as you consider your candidates for counsel for the upcoming vendor negotiations, please keep my skills and accomplishments in mind:

- Accomplished contract negotiator and manager, with international work-location experience, and over ten successful years developing, drafting, negotiating, and managing sales and other customer-related contracts. Typical contracts include distribution, reseller, OEM, and government.

- Negotiated all time charter business with major oil companies and traders. Supervised all spot charter negotiations in conjunction with operations, legal, engineering, insurance, financial, and personnel departments. Negotiated eight overseas new building construction contracts in excess of $400 million.

- Attended Karrass Effective Negotiating Techniques Seminar.

- Managed $200 million in government contracts and $600 million in proposal efforts during FY04. Responsible for full life cycle negotiation and administration of federal government solicitations and contracts for AT&T's government service offerings.

- Administered and negotiated commercial and government contracts, including software and technology licenses, in accordance with applicable procurement, FAR, DFAR, ITAR, and GSA requirements.

- Responsible for analysis, negotiation, and administration of contracts for services, supplies, construction, and research and development for activities at various Department of Defense, Federal Laboratories, and private organizations.

I am certain these accomplishments will support my lead candidacy. Please call me anytime you have any questions.

Alicia Paramo

To: Tricia Boyle

From: Patrick Dudash

Date: October 12, 20__

Subject: Follow-up to Interview

Tricia, while at Porter Merchandising, I was the lead negotiator for corporate contracts, statements of work, amendments for outsourcing of IT and finance and accounting services, acquisition of information technology, professional services, and outsourced call centers, both offshore and onshore logistics, and materials management services:

❑ Highly effective in reducing costs for goods and services and reduced risk by negotiating preferential contract terms.

❑ Optimized the corporation's supplier base by consolidating internal customer requirements and negotiating beneficial pricing and commercial terms.

In addition, I participated on the negotiating team for the largest alliance in company history: limited strategic alliance ($800 million investment in the company as part of the overall agreement).

❑ Reviewed over 200 proposals and worked on 10 teams focused on specific deals (partnerships, strategic equity investments, acquisition, etc.).

❑ Represented The Limited corporate development as an advisor to business units and Internet team—targeting, reviewing, negotiating, performing due diligence on projects related to the Internet, devices, applications, and new partnerships and technologies.

❑ Managed transaction and project pipeline process as well as the unsolicited proposal evaluation process based on The Limited's strategic priorities for all business units and business development activities.

Please expect my call early next week so we can discuss this in more detail.

Best regards,

Patrick Dudash

CAROL JOHNSON

124 Shawnee Lane, Drayton Plains, MI 48888
cj@wdr.com

May 1, 20__

Mr. Rick Werner
Senior Vice President, Cocoa Corporation
999 John Carpenter Freeway
Las Colinas, TX 72222

Dear Rick:

I am excited about the offer you extended on April 28, and look forward to accepting it. I feel confident I will make a significant contribution to the growth and profitability of Cocoa's service organization over the short and long term. The terms you have described in the offer are acceptable, with a few minor requests.

Base Salary: $81,000 annually
The research I've done on comparable salaries and cost-of-living differences between Dallas and Detroit show that a base salary of $102,000 would be the market value of my experience for this position in Dallas. The current offer of $81,000 would result in a dramatic reduction in living standard in making the move from Detroit to Dallas. Based on the above, I would like you to consider as a compromise a base salary of $93,000.

Bonus Opportunity: 5% of quarterly team results above stated quotas
Because I expect to have an immediate impact on both cost savings and improved service, I would like to suggest increasing the bonus percentage to 6% of results above quota.

Relocation Package: Your relocation offer of reimbursement up to $10,000 for my move to Dallas is a little low. That will cover my packing and actual moving expenses, but not the real estate cost of selling my home. While I do not expect Cocoa to buy my home as part of the move package, is there anything that can be done to relieve me of some of the cost of selling my home? My home is valued at $225,000, and 6% of that is $13,500.

Stock Option Plan: Eligible after one year of service
Considering that this is standard policy for all employees, I understand this may not be negotiable. However, given the immediate impact I am sure I will make, I'd love to participate sooner.

Benefits Package: Health and associated insurance
Looks good!

Start Date: May 23
Pending resolution of the travel and relocation issues, this can work.

Please give these requests some consideration and let's discuss them in a couple days. I am sure you will realize the benefits of my contribution, and I am even willing to put some of these terms on hold pending one year of successful employment prior to the benefit (on the relocation aid request).

Sincerely,

Carol Johnson

Michael Lane
101 Eagles Way, Odessa, FL 33556   ml@eway.com

January 20, 20__

Ms. Emily Sloane
Tudisco Resources, Inc.
14 Orlando Way
Orlando, FL 33409

Dear Ms. Sloane:

Thank you for your offer letter. I am excited at the prospect of joining Tudisco Resources in the coming weeks. I believe there are a few items to clarify, prior to providing you with a formal acceptance.

The compensation plan calls for a straight commission arrangement, and that is not like the plans I have been on in the past. I am very confident I will be able to exceed past earnings, but the initial period until the business ramps up is my only concern.

I am requesting a signing bonus or "bridge" wage to help me until the business begins to become billed. This is not unusual in the industry and would make my decision to come on board much easier. This will also provide Tudisco the opportunity to share some of the risk in this process and demonstrate short-term good faith toward what I hope will be a long-term relationship of success, productivity, and increased profitability.

The other item of concern is clarification of your health-care benefits and the timing. I would appreciate it if you could send me further information about your health-care program.

Please let me know what you think we can do about my requests, and we can talk in a couple days. Once we work this out, I will give my current employer my resignation notice.

Thanks, and I look forward to speaking with you soon.

Sincerely,

Michael Lane

To: Aaron Grant

From: Savannah Harrington

Date: May 21, 20__

Subject: Offer Letter

Thank you for the time that we were able to spend together last week. I was encouraged by the invitation to join Trinity Medical as pharmaceutical specialist. This is a position I have been seeking, and I am excited about joining the team.

Based on the information that you gave me, there are a couple things that need clarification prior to my accepting the offer. Can you please e-mail or fax me details on the following items?

- Insurance benefit details, timing, and plan overviews

- 401K and company matching programs, and timing of participation

- Detailed explanation of the at-risk portion of the comp plan based on drug sales

As I consider the move from Grant Chemicals to Trinity, I do need to take into account the compensation impact. We talked about it, and based on our conversations I am confident this will work out, but I'd like to see the plan in writing and with your realistic expectations prior to accepting the offer. I really do need to have a realistic chance to earn over $90,000 through my base and bonus potential.

Thanks, Aaron! I look forward to hearing from you soon.

Savannah

Pamela Waterson

101 Eagles Way, Odessa, FL 33556

April 30, 20___

Ms. Maria Lane
Robert Haver Associates
14 Orlando Way
Orlando, FL 33409

Dear Ms. Lane:

My fifteen years' experience in managing multiple projects simultaneously, including the ability to work under pressure, meet tight deadlines, and utilize problem-solving skills to ensure that projects meet stated goals and objectives, is a very good fit for your operations management position.

My success lies in leading revenue generation programs, with particular skill in managing multiple projects simultaneously from concept to completion. This skill enables me to consistently bring projects to a successful finish on time and on budget.

In 2005 I was promoted to lead the project management team. I managed all aspects of the division's business and systems projects by preparing and managing project plans, scheduling and facilitating status meetings, and evaluating and analyzing cost-benefit relationships.

IIf you are ever going to self-promote, the time to do it is in the interviewing process. I really am a committed professional and I understand the importance of being organized and keeping things organized for those around me.

Sincerely,

Pamela Waterson

BARRY HOSKOWT

1 Madison Way, Irvine, CA 91111 949.555.1111
bht@mmm.com

June 3, 20__

Ms. Sally Degner
Senior Director, IT Systems
999 John Carpenter Freeway
Las Colinas, TX 72222

Dear Ms. Degner:

As a principle at Arrow Consulting, I recognize that project management for marketing programs is a cornerstone of successful engagements and building a client base. I am experienced in all areas of targeted marketing, retail management, and ad production and printing, and am skillful at managing multiple projects simultaneously.

My organization led a strategic marketing plan for the company, researched and evaluated new safety software, provided detailed case research and accident reconstruction support for ongoing litigation, and published press releases, all of which contributed to a successful IPO in 2006.

Working with cross-functional teams, I achieve win-win outcomes through strong organizational skills with an acute attention to detail, the ability to multitask, and excellent analytical, follow-through, and decision-making skills.

As managing account executive, I am responsible for marketing, coordinating, and managing vendor services for large corporate accounts. My group represented multiple regional vendor services, specializing in worker's compensation, auto, medical malpractice, and disability insurance, requiring excellent organizational skills and project planning.

From my understanding of what you are seeking, my accomplishments closely align with your objectives. Feel free to contact me via phone or e-mail at your earliest opportunity.

Sincerely,

Barry Hoskowt

To: Debbie Pekar

From: Steve Miller

Date: December 19, 20__

Subject: Interview Follow-up

Debbie, thank you so much for the time you spent with me yesterday. I thoroughly enjoyed learning more about HAW and your objectives. I know organizational skills are mission-critical to you, so please let me take a few moments to reinforce the points I made in our meeting.

o   At Cisco Systems I managed the partner program support, including the production and distribution of electronic partner packages, multiple collateral projects (data sheets and division overview brochure), trade show collateral, and signage requirements.

o   A successful coordinator effectively manages integrated marketing programs with limited resources, from development through implementation to program reporting and analysis. I am experienced at consulting with teams to understand their needs, uncovering opportunities, and recommending creative ideas and solutions. I also have proven skills in organizing, prioritizing, and managing multiple projects simultaneously on time and within budget.

o   My sales support organization interfaced with three regional sales centers and field marketing to develop projects targeting installed customers to increase customer loyalty. Under my leadership we developed and managed integrated marcom projects from concept to completion.

I will follow up with you by Tuesday of next week. Enjoy your weekend!

Steve

To: Omar Omari

From: Jimmy Vrable

Date: May 18, 20__

Subject: Presentation Skills Highlights and General Thoughts

Omar, oral communication skills are critical to the success of individuals and their organizations. This is equally true whether you are communicating one to one, or one to two hundred and fifty. A good presentation has the power to deliver your message and the emotional force to move your audience to new ways of thinking and/or behaving.

I possess accomplished oral presentation skills: I create presentations that excite and inform, and I effectively deliver speeches, whether prepared or extemporaneous. I have skills in developing and delivering a training curriculum including presentations and workbooks. I really enjoy doing this, and it shows.

With respect to presentations:

▲   I am an engaging speaker and seminar leader, sales presenter, and technical management liaison.
▲   I enjoy a natural ability to work with others, influence C-level decision making, and promote company products and services to a wide range of targeted prospects, alliance partners, and vendor leaders.
▲   I can create and present executive-level seminars and workshops, generate goodwill and future interest at corporate trade shows, and author specialized articles and procedural documentation.
▲   I establish quick rapport with coworkers, professionals, and staff. I exercise diplomacy and tact, and I enjoy a reputation for relational excellence.

Omar, this really is my passion and it shows. I will be forwarding to you some of my nonproprietary presentations and will walk you through them in our meeting later this week.

Thanks again for your consideration.

Jimmy

To: Walter Johnston

From: Cary Temple

Date: February 1, 20__

Subject: Live Presentation Experience

Walter, I believe there is nothing so effective as a live presentation in a variety of venues, including trade shows and conferences, to create exciting buzz. I am regularly requested to speak at industry trade conferences, including CES in Las Vegas each January.

In addition to external presentations, I have communicated compliance results to corporate management through oral presentations and written reports:

▲ Conducted corporate staff presentations and creative employee training seminars

▲ Responsible for new product presentations and sales techniques throughout California

Prior to my employment in the consumer products industry, I gave over a thousand lectures, primarily for Ford Motor Company, Fidelity, and Anderson Consulting. In 2004 I was recognized by *Marketing and Sales* magazine as one of the top ten speakers in the United States. The WTC in Dallas has ranked me as "America's number one motivational technology speaker." I have also been featured in many magazines and have written three books published by McGraw-Hill.

I am sure there is much I can share with your firm and learn along the way.

Cary

To: Edward Bellerman

From: Laura Lilienthal

Date: December 1, 20__

Subject: Public and Motivational Speaking Experience

Edward, I wrote a keynote speech for a motivational speaker at the shareholder convention for DRW in 2008. I doubled the original content through extensive research and interviews. After countless revisions to make the tone and texture of the language sound consistent with the speaker's personal style, it received excellent audience feedback and a repeat invitation for the speaker.

I frequently speak to audiences that range from 100 to 2,500 people, and I speak to an average of 15,000 people a year. As a marketing/motivational speaker, I participated in training classes through the delivery of entertaining and informative lectures to middle and high school students. Topics include those that encourage and support self-confidence, social skills, and the like. Audience numbers ranged from 30 to more than 300.

Preparing and delivering exciting and informative lectures/workshops on a variety of topics with emphasis on positive thinking and personal empowerment is my passion. Some topics of discussion include interviewing techniques, clarifying goals, personal life mission statement, believing in yourself, and living your full potential. Below are some other areas that fall within the discipline I thoroughly enjoy and in which I thrive:

- Management: Known for a contagious passion for excellence, a talent for resourceful business solutions, and motivational leadership. Effectively use an empowering, participatory management style that encourages accountability, teamwork, and the continuous improvement of desired results.

- Team Building: In business, organizational leadership, training and education, recognized for ability to merge dissimilar people into cohesive teams with common focus.

- Communication: Challenging motivational speaker. Excellent communication skills; experienced in motivating and inspiring both large and small groups of individuals in common vision and purpose.

Thanks for thinking of me to lead this project and help you turn your sales organization up another notch.

Laura Lilienthal

David Heintzelman

3 Dallas Way
Grapevine, TX 75555
(972) 555-5555

March 4, 20___

Ms. Debbie Caskey
430 Houston Way
Houston, TX 78444

Dear Ms. Caskey:

Based on the program manager description you provided, strong problem-solving skills are very important to this position. That's good, because I consider this one of my inherent strengths!

As a project manager with P&G, I demonstrated a strong background in methods and time studies for setting production standards. In 2007 I did a rotation in the West Virginia plant and managed the start-up of a new state-of-the-art distribution center. My references would describe me as particularly effective in assessing and resolving employee conflicts and organizational problems, allowing for increased productivity.

As a successful project manager and problem solver, one must develop strategic relationships with various department heads and suppliers. This facilitates communication and problem resolution within the organization and improves the flow of information and overall efficiencies.

Success in this role requires strong interpersonal and communication capabilities in working with a wide range of personnel at all levels to gain valuable insight, avoid potential problems, and facilitate the timely completion of projects.

This is beginning to appear more and more like a good mutual fit. I am looking forward to discussing it with you in more detail next week.

Sincerely,

David Heintzelman

Lisa Councilman

1013 Westlake Circle
Kansas City, KS 00000
(816) 555-5555

June 29, 20__

Ms. Angela Redding
900 Main Street, Suite 400
St. Louis, MO 00000

Dear Ms. Redding:

Because problem solving is so important to the success of the operations manager position we discussed, please allow me to take a few moments to highlight some of my career accomplishments in this area. We did discuss some of these points, but I would like to highlight them once again as you think about the applicability of my accomplishments to your position needs:

- A veteran production manager; experienced with quality assurance, problem solving, streamlining processes, and optimizing production workflow. Extensive experience in project management, creating intuitive business collateral, Internet promotion, and developing proactive marketing strategies.

- Strengths are solving problems, analyzing the symptoms, identifying what is wrong, and finding the solution. Also strong in conceptual intellect. Ability to move beyond limiting questions and to nurture problem-solving ideas through each of four phases of creative problem solving.

- Strategic thinker; Ten years solving design, communication, and process problems.

- Management/problem solving/communication skills. Managed all print and presentation projects with over a 95% on-time rate. Handled project tracking, system/file management, estimating, budget/billing, vendor billing, and liaisons with all vendors.

- Administration, planning, and problem solving: Oversee multiple tasks with varying priorities; work with many departments within an organization to ensure smooth operation, productivity, and marketing; identify areas of improvement; research; and develop and implement improved procedures.

I will call you Wednesday to follow up on our meeting. Thanks again for your consideration!

Lisa Councilman

To: Marilena Westwood

From: Marty Quarto

Date: September 8, 20__

Subject: Organizational Changes and Associate Impacts

Marilena, under my leadership we initiated a turnaround with a complete restaffing of our entire marketing organization. We recruited qualified personnel, introduced internal training programs, redesigned core processes, enhanced technologies, and created a sophisticated and responsive organization.

We also provided the executive team and senior operating management with meaningful financial data, which kept their initiatives closer to our financial objectives.

Our organization also introduced a series of personnel and executive incentive plans that enhanced performance and accountability.

In relocating our corporate offices, field organization structure, and associated equipment for 9,300 employees in less than 120 days, we trimmed a year-over-year cost structure from 17% of gross revenues down to 13.6%, which improved our net income status by over 2%.

Overall, the two-year project was a huge success and something I am sure I can implement at OCR.

I'm looking forward to discussing this with you next time we speak.

Thanks again!

Marty

To: Carol Polarter

From: Michael Porter

Date: September 8, 20__

Subject: Organizational and Process Changes We Discussed

Carol, as the senior lead management consultant to Citibank's Business Division, I was the functional director lead in reengineering design, development, testing, business analysis, and implementation of Citibank's enterprise migration and conversion. I provided senior management with direction in gap analysis, data architectural design and functionality, vendor relationship decisions, and implementation guidance.

The work included process reengineering, commercial markets:

❑ Responsible for building an infrastructure to support new marketing initiatives, integrating traditional financial services into bundled offerings for the Prospect Segment directorate.

❑ Led a major reengineering project to automate the marketing program release processes, including an intranet marketing program offer and message template generation system, an automated data feed to all downstream processes, and a redesigned database algorithm to optimize table size and vendor performance. This project dramatically reduced marketing program cycle time and recycle errors.

These changes had a dramatic positive impact on our financial results in an ever-changing and contracting environment.

Please expect my call on Friday to discuss this in more detail.

Michael

To: Richard Littlerer

From: Angela Evans

Date: July 2, 20__

Subject: IT Organizational Changes

Richard, you asked me to send you a quick note to highlight the changes under my leadership and the associated impacts. I was credited with reengineering IT operations and establishing a new enterprise computing environment within nine months.

- Created and implemented IT processes, procedures, and standards.
- Planned and designed network and topology architecture. Directed teams in reengineering network infrastructures and migrating company from token ring to ethernet topology. Managed the implementation of WAN to ensure appropriate data access and integration throughout all locations, including firewall and security strategies.

This action promoted renewed commitment across the IT division to the change management process and practices, doubling the level of regular participation in weekly change management meetings, greatly improving interdepartmental coordination, with regard to middle- to high-visibility changes.

We developed a process for production test, implementation, and change management as well as security policy, systems performance process and reporting, migration process, and redundant facilities environments.

A task force I led also evaluated helpdesk functions, focusing on structure and strategy, perception and performance, methodologies and procedures, staffing and education, systems, and technology and management reporting. We instituted all change management initiatives to improve these functions.

Finally, we consulted with customers and managed multiple projects such as information security and access control, enterprise change management, disaster recovery and business continuity planning, and new core network build-out support.

I can expand on this next time we speak, but you requested some bullet points in writing prior to that.

Please let me know if you need anything else.

Angela

Kris Mills
1 PR Way, Puerto Rico 00000 (487) 555-5555

April 2, 20__

Brenda Walsh
BW Securities
16111 Blue Ridge Circle
Palm Beach, FL 33440

Dear Ms. Walsh:

Time management is a giant skill for a successful person, in any discipline. No question. So many people think they have it, and so few do. Time management is all about exercising expertise in finding out how much time is worth, concentrating on the right things, deciding work priorities, planning to solve a problem, tackling the right tasks first through prioritized to-do lists, and executing the plan in a timely manner.

Ms. Walsh, I am very organized, detail oriented, and self motivated, with excellent time management, prioritization, and multiple task/project coordination skills. I have a strong work ethic and professional attitude emphasizing reliability, integrity, teamwork, and the willingness to work as necessary to get the job done.

Last year I was certified in time management through a Franklin Time Management Course. Success has so much to do with prioritizing tasks, organizing and coordinating activities, managing time, setting and achieving goals, meeting deadlines, developing relationships, and establishing procedures.

This year we sponsored an 80:20 program at Toyota, which argues that typically 80% of unfocused effort generates only 20% of results. The remaining 80% of results are achieved with only 20% of the effort. My team led the initiative to improve time management skills of 670+ employees. The result was a measurable productivity improvement of over 12%.

I would be eager to speak with you in more detail about this.

Sincerely,

Kris Mills

HELEN KRAMER

1 Melbourne Way, Denver, CO 33333 303.555.1111
hk@spd.net

October 2, 20__

Mr. Mike Hannigan
1 Pikes Peak
Colorado Springs, CO 00000

Dear Mr. Hannigan:

I understand you have a penchant for your team members using time wisely. I agree with you about the effective use of time management and understanding the key principles of time management to become more efficient. The essence of time management can be expressed in five major points:

1. Know the big picture.
2. Understand the difference between urgent and important.
3. Learn to think and act in a proactive way.
4. Use weekly planning as your major tool.
5. Avoid time wasters.

To me, time management is the ability to manage multiple assignments and maintain quality of service under fast-paced conditions. In order to meet the research and development timetable for the ZBOX offering, my team employed outstanding time management and resource allocation skills to coordinate multiple tasks while maintaining strong quality focus.

In fact, my entire team was certified in the Active Listening Course, the Decker Communication Course, and the Franklin Time Management Course.

I am looking forward to expanding on this the next time we speak.

Sincerely,

Helen Kramer

Chris Zach

1 Carrollton Way, Chicago, IL 75243 cz@rentway.org 314 555 0000

March 12, 20__

Rick Mears
Mears and Associates
202 Waterway
Chicago, IL 75000

Dear Mr. Mears:

Effective project planning and time management really do go hand in hand in delivering a complex initiative on time and on budget. I was involved in training the clients' project team and determining global template functionality for the global project team in the USA.

My duties included project plan preparation, progress reporting, training of the local project team, determining local requirements, identification and specification of system interfaces, final configuration of the system, and system and acceptance testing. Modules configured and implemented were PA, PD, Training and Events, Recruitment, and Time Management.

We effectively used advanced and disciplined project planning experience to list tasks, prioritize them, and map out execution of all them. Our discipline included avoiding procrastination, using time wisely, planning exceptionally, and employing the use of the Covey planning system. Following are skills I contributed to the effort:

❑ Provided relevant and timely sales and time management.
❑ Conducted training needs assessments to determine training shortfalls and needs.
❑ Attended several sales and time management courses (Covey, Franklin, Career Path); developed and conducted specific training courses that addressed the needs of our business.
❑ Provided consultation services in time management training to two corporations.

I am very interested in bringing these skills and disciplines to your organization. Please expect a call from me on Tuesday to discuss this in more detail.

Sincerely,

Chris Zach

Paul Cartney
1 Caroline Way ▪ Christopher, TX 75555 ▪ pw@tt.org

August 12, 20__

Mr. Michael Stone
Senior Editor, JWA
14 Park Avenue
New York, NY 11111

Dear Mr. Stone:

I am indeed very interested in the marketing communications manager position we discussed this morning. To be proficient at this position, a strong competency is a critical skill to possess.

Below are some of my career highlights in this discipline:

❑ Wrote preview briefs for two clients for the CES Show in January 2005.

❑ Built briefing books for clients utilizing information obtained from various sources.

❑ Took the initiative to sort out the magazine lists and ed cal lists, giving my management the chance to refocus their top tier and thus giving their clients a better service level.

❑ Worked with creative directors, training manager(s) to develop, implement, create, and design staff instruction manuals, newsletters, Web pages, policy and procedure manuals, and announcements to publicize various training programs using Excel, PowerPoint, Word, and Lotus Notes.

❑ Assisted in layout design and production of printed materials, including newsletters, brochures, slides, graphs, and other visual PowerPoint presentation materials. Created Excel/Access spreadsheets, database, word processing, and graphics computer software programs. Conceptualized and designed layouts and formats for brochures, annual reports, direct mail, newsletters, advertisements, and corporate imaging.

I am certain this is a very good mutual fit. I am looking forward to the next step in the interview process.

Have a great weekend!

Paul Cartney

Michelle Lane
101 Bobby Way • Detroit, MI 48221 • gs123@httryw.com

February 8, 20__

Mick Lennon
Lennon & Associates
1 Birmingham Street
Birmingham, MI 48207

Dear Mr. Lennon:

I am very excited about the copywriter position available at Lennon & Associates. Lennon is one of the most creative agencies on Madison Avenue, and joining that team is a breathtaking career prospect for me.

As I mentioned, I am highly resourceful and possess strong merchandising and visual presentation skills. My accomplishments validate a strong attention to detail and a keen sense of color, balance, and scale. I also love to expand on creative ideas and concepts.

Additional skills I developed at R&R include:

- Proposal writing
- Presentations
- Technology auditing
- Contract writing (including statement of work)
- Client communications, product branding, product rollouts (creative and tactical implementation), communication templates, proposal style guides, process documentation, and ad campaign development
- Collateral development: wrote copy for marketing pieces including but not limited to product sheets, press releases, brochures and flyers, ad copy, board reports, and client communications
- Proposal writing: for various business lines, effective content with high-impact responses, high-quality proposal packaging, and strategic messaging and targeting
- Media and public relations: developed strategies to heighten awareness and visibility in the industry, speechwriting, and media collateral and kits

Mr. Lennon, I really am a perfect fit for this position. I will send over a sample of work I have created.

I am looking forward to seeing you next Tuesday to meet with your team for the 360 interviews.

Sincerely,

Michelle Lane

Brittany Avery

I Castle Way, Fort Worth, TX 77777 817.555.1111

May 19, 20___

Avery Johnson
Nokai Communications
Irving, TX 77777

Dear Mr. Johnson:

The Web support role for which you are recruiting is indeed a very good fit for both of us, at least based on what you presented when we spoke earlier. Here are some accomplishments that I believe align me closely with your objectives.

For the past two years, I served as Web editor responsible for writing and maintaining content including service offering descriptions, value propositions, FAQs, news items, and seed content for the online community.

❑ Managed content administration for the Web site including updates, revisions, and posting of new material (ATG/Interwoven content management system).
❑ Redeveloped Web sites including page design, site structure, and navigation.
❑ Researched, developed, and wrote Web-based interactive business training (included instructional story and material, quizzes and tutoring, expert interviews and audio, and glossary and FAQs); conceptualized and worked with tech staff to develop a multimedia component that reinforced the instructional material.
❑ Developed informational resource articles on work/life issues; identified new areas and ideas for development including resources, tools, and potential alliance partners.

From a writing and editing discipline:

❑ Research, drafting, and editing for book *Understanding Financial Statements: A Journalist's Guide*, published by Marion Street Press.
❑ Former teacher of writing seminars at Newberry Library and Latin School Adult Programs.
❑ Author of nine articles that have appeared in national trade magazines including the interviewing of subject matter experts.
❑ Editor of employee newsletters.
❑ Research, writing, and editing of public communications (policy statements, speeches, correspondence, and ceremonial messages).
❑ Writing and editing of reports (a client deliverable) covering investigative findings, conclusions, and recommendations.

I will call you on Wednesday to discuss our next steps. Thanks again for your consideration.

Sincerely,

Brittany Avery

14

Contact During and After the Interview Process

Opting to write a follow-up letter is probably not a deciding factor in whether you will move forward in the job search process, assuming there is mutual interest between the candidate and the hiring manager. However, there was a time last year when it did make a difference.

I was interviewing two different managers for the same position. They were equally matched, and I was having a difficult time selecting which one to make an offer to. After I had interviewed both of them, one candidate sent me a follow-up e-mail and actually recapped a portion of our meeting and addressed some things we had discussed. That was followed up by a call two days later. The other candidate went dark after the interview. The candidate who made the diligent follow-up was offered the position, simply because I felt she might be hungrier and wanted the position more than the other.

Consider thank-you letters as follow-up sales letters. This is an opportunity to restate why you want the job and what your qualifications are, and, most important, address any concerns the hiring manager discussed in the interview. It is also a perfect opportunity to review anything that the recruiter or hiring manager neglected to ask or that you neglected to answer as well as you would have liked.

Here are some follow-up letter tips:

- If you were interviewed by a group of people, send each of them a specific note and make each note different. In case they compare the notes, they should not merely be copied-and-pasted versions of the same letter.

- Proofread the letter for typos and grammatical excellence, as discussed in Chapter 3.
- Send the letter (usually an e-mail) within 24 hours
- When accepting an offer of employment, state in writing your understanding of the terms of employment. Your acceptance letter is not a legal contract, but it will come in handy if any question ever arises over the terms of your employment. Address the letter to the person who offered you the position. If that person is in human resources, then copy the hiring manager. Articulate that you look forward to filling this new position, and recap one or two elements of the job.

To: Michael David

From: Lisa Ramirez

Date: October 2, 20__

Subject: Offer Letter Accepted!

As we discussed on the phone, I am very pleased to accept the position of marketing manager with Qwest Communications. Thank you for the opportunity. I am excited at the prospect of having a positive impact on the organization and working with everyone on the Qwest team.

As we discussed, my starting salary will be $73,000 and associated benefits will be provided after ninety days following my first day of employment.

I look forward to starting employment on October 13. If there is any additional information or paperwork you need prior to then, please let me know.

Again, thank you.

Lisa Ramirez

156—ACCEPT OFFER

To: Lisa Councilman
From: Ally Heathrow
Date: June 21, 20__
Subject: Position Accepted!

Lisa, I would like to accept the position as the district manager for The Hat. As we agreed, my first day will be July 1.

The terms of employment as detailed in your offer letter dated June 20 are completely acceptable; this is a wonderful opportunity, and I am eager to begin.

Yesterday we also discussed my primary emphasis for the first three to four months, and I fully understand and am in complete agreement.

First, I need to complete the staffing at the lowest-performing stores.

Second, I need to develop a training plan for those employees we plan to retain, to improve their skill level.

Third, I need to improve the expectations and accountability of the store managers in the running of their business.

To assist with my first priority, could you please make sure we are running advertisements and circulating the message that we need staff, to shorten the cycle when I start? Also, if I could get a copy of the training and personnel evaluations of the teams as soon as possible, I'd be happy to look them over to familiarize myself with them ahead of time.

Lisa, I believe we will accomplish some great things together. Please call on me anytime prior to my start date.

Ally

To: Grace Matherly
From: Kevin Kahlden
Date: February 5, 20__
Subject: Offer Letter

Grace, I am pleased to accept your verbal offer of employment to join your team on February 17 as the food and beverage manager. We agreed my compensation package includes a base salary of $63,000, participation in the company's health plan, 401K participation immediately, and participation in an annual bonus program.

Could you please set aside a full day during my first week to set objectives and develop a plan of priorities in addition to the routine with which my team now operates?

I am very excited about working with you and the rest of the team. Together, I am certain we can significantly improve the operational efficiencies and cost controls we discussed in the business.

Looking forward to the 17th!

Kevin

Becky Hiebert

1 Plaza Space
Kansas City, KS 00000
(816) 555-0000

August 12, 20___

Mr. Paul Kramer
Director, The Store
1 Metcalf Place
Overland Park, KS 00000

Dear Mr. Kramer:

It was certainly wonderful news when you called this afternoon to offer me the position as buyer for The Store. Please consider this letter my formal acceptance.

I am pleased to accept your offer at a salary of $71,000 annually.

As we agreed, my starting date will be September 1.

I also understand that I will receive full company benefits upon my first day of employment, and 401K contribution eligibility after ninety days of employment.

Thank you again, Mr. Kramer, for offering me this wonderful opportunity, and do let me know if I can do anything in advance of my start date to facilitate the paperwork or whether there are any areas you'd like me to be reading up on.

What a delight it will be to work with you and The Store team!

Sincerely,

Becky Hiebert

To: Jeff Klein

From: Courtney Jacobson

Date: April 11, 20__

Subject: Offer Letter Received

Dear Mr. Klein:

I am acknowledging your letter offering me the health administrator position with Trinity Medical, Inc. Thank you very much for offering me this exciting opportunity. I understand the terms of your offer and am certain I will be able to give you a response by your requested deadline of April 13.

I appreciate your allowing me ample time to consider your offer so that I can be sure my decision will be in the best interests of both my career goals and the needs of your corporation.

In the meantime, should I have any questions, I will call you. Please do not hesitate to call me if I can provide you with any needed information.

Sincerely,

Courtney

Kate Marano
1111 Tampa Road • Oldsmar, FL 33556 • km@yahaa.com • 813-555-1212

March 2, 20__

Richard Jacobson
Director of Recruiting
Limited Brands, Inc.
rj@ltd.com

Dear Mr. Jacobson:

Thank you for offering me the opportunity to join The Limited as a brand manager. I am very pleased to accept your offer and look forward to jumping right in to the fray and making a significant contribution as soon as possible. I am particularly excited to be joining the brand equity research focus groups we discussed.

I am honored that The Limited feels that I am the right person to lead your branding discipline and am confident that I can deliver the results you are seeking. As I mentioned in our phone conversation Monday, I keep in frequent touch with what similar retailers are doing and will spend some time between now and my start date familiarizing myself with all the retailers in The Limited family.

I will wait to hear from Tony, your new-hire manager, for the logistics associated with my start date. I look forward to working with you and the rest of the team in the coming weeks. Thanks once again!

Sincerely,

Kate Marano

Chris Kramer

3000 Shawnee Lane
Drayton Plains, MI 48888
(248) 555-5555

March 21, 20__

Ms. Carol Houston
Cameo Rehabilitation
1900 Main Street
Clarkston, MI 48888

Dear Ms. Houston:

I want to thank you for the privilege of joining your staff as dealer support manager. Your flexibility and cooperation as we worked out some of the final details was encouraging. Thank you for making every effort to make the pending transition a smooth one.

Considering that Cameo is a competitor of HealthSouth, and in that Cameo seeks to maintain goodwill and a high level of integrity within the industry, it should be communicated, if asked, that neither you nor anyone from Cameo reached out to me as a prospective employee. When I identified the opportunity with Cameo, it was my initiative and interest that brought us together, and I am happy to ensure that action is shared.

If you need me to do anything to clarify this, please let me know. I will communicate this message in writing to HealthSouth upon my resignation. Thanks, and I am looking forward to joining the Cameo team!

Respectfully yours,

Chris Kramer

Christopher Silko

14 Davison, Detroit, MI 48888 313.555.0000

February 12, 20__

Mr. Thomas Redwing
Redwing and Associates, Ltd.
21 Peachtree Street
Atlanta, GA 33333

Dear Mr. Redwing:

This letter will serve as my formal acceptance of your offer to join Redwing and Associates as director of business development. I understand and accept the conditions of employment, which were explained in Helen Kramer's offer letter.

I will contact Helen this week to request any forms I might need to complete for your new-hire paperwork prior to my starting date. Also, I will schedule the drug test today. I would appreciate your forwarding any industry information that you think might accelerate my learning curve prior to my start date.

Yesterday I tendered my resignation at Delphia and worked out a mutually acceptable notice time of two weeks, which should allow me ample time to be prepared for our agreed-upon start date of March 1.

You and your team have been most helpful throughout my interview process. I am very excited at the prospect of joining the Redwing team and look forward to many new challenges. Thank you for your confidence and support.

Yours truly,

Christopher Silko

Cynthia Hernandez

1 Brady Drive, Boston, MA 00000
(508) 555-5555

January 18, 20__

Eileen Simon
Director of Human Resources, MMNA
909 Dallas Parkway
Dallas, TX 75240

Dear Ms. Simon:

I enjoyed interviewing with you during your recruiting visit to the University of Texas on January 15. The management trainee program we discussed sounds both challenging and rewarding, and I look forward to the next step of visiting others at MMNA at your corporate office.

I will be graduating in April with a bachelor's degree in finance. Through my education and experience I've gained many skills, and I took the most rigorous coursework available within the finance major. As well, I have studied and followed the industry and am as aware as a student could be of the professional expectations this position and discipline require. I sincerely believe my education and work experience would complement MMNA's management trainee program.

I have enclosed a copy of my college transcript and a list of references that you requested. Thanks again for the opportunity to meet with you. The interview served to reinforce my strong interest in becoming a part of your team. I can be reached at (508) 555-5555, and will call you next Wednesday to discuss next steps.

Sincerely,

Cynthia Hernandez

Larry Orlando
1908 Shawnee Lane, Drayton Plains, MI 48280   (248) 555-5555

March 31, 20___

Alicia Paramo
Director of Operations, UOU
1022 Walton Boulevard
Rochester, MI 48888

Dear Ms. Paramo:

Thank you for the opportunity to visit with you and see your campus earlier this week. The tour of the campus and the three meetings I had were very interesting and have motivated me even more to pursue an opportunity with UOU.

I was particularly impressed with the openness of the culture there and what really seemed like the highest morale I've seen anywhere. Michael Joseph was very thorough in explaining the organization to me, and I will be following up directly with him to express my appreciation. Based on the work I have done at UDM, I believe there is much I can offer in terms of new ideas while in turn learning much from your organization—really a mutual win for us both.

Again, thank you for your hospitality and for all your efforts to arrange my visit. Having seen your corporation and many of the talented people there, I am all the more enthused about the career opportunity that UOU offers. I look forward to speaking with you soon, and will follow up on Friday.

Sincerely,

Larry Orlando

Bobby Shanahan
1 Charlotte Way
Norman, NC 11111
704.555.5555

August 3, 20__

Ms. Jill Kabana
Quality Assurance
1 Main Street, Suite A
Charlotte, NC 55555

Dear Ms. Kabana:

I submitted a letter of application and a resume earlier this month for the program manager position. To date, I have not heard from your office, and I would like to confirm receipt of my application and reiterate my interest in the job.

I am very interested in working at Quality Assurance, and I believe my skills and experience would be worthy of exploring to see if there is a mutual fit.

If necessary, I would be glad to resend my application materials or to provide any further information you might need regarding my candidacy. I will call you Thursday to see if we can set up a few moments to talk. I'd love to be able to meet in person, and I believe there is a strong enough fit on paper to warrant it for both of us.

Thanks again, Ms. Kabana.

Sincerely,

Bobby Shanahan

John Harrison
1 Carrollton Way, Carrollton, TX 75243   jharrison@ccc.com   214 555 0000

March 12, 20__

Richard Wyman
Snelling and Snelling
45 LBJ Freeway
Dallas, TX 75240

Dear Mr. Wyman:

I'm writing to let you know that I am still very much interested in the group manager of marketing position we discussed last week. With the cutting-edge offerings of your client Centennial, this represents a great fit for both of us.

You mentioned their interest in breaking into data services via the WiFi technology as one way to increase Centennial's market share. Just as a reminder, I do have some experience in the broadband space, marketing in both B2B and B2C environments. In fact, I have been researching to see what other competitors in the field are doing in this market segment. With no other wireless competitors, there is a wide-open field for Centennial to be first to market and establish itself as an industry leader.

I will continue this research, and really want to come in again to discuss how I might apply this information to Centennial's long-term plans. Please call me if you need any additional data for my application; otherwise, please expect my call this Friday.

Sincerely,

John Harrison

HELEN KRAMER

1 Melbourne Way, Denver, CO 33333 303.555.1111
hk@spd.net

October 2, 20__

Mr. Mike Hannigan
Chase Morgan
1 Pikes Peak
Colorado Springs, CO 00000

Dear Mr. Hannigan:

It was a pleasure meeting with you last Thursday to discuss the director of client operations position. I appreciate the time you spent discussing the growth planned in this area and my potential fit in the organization. The ranking you enjoy in the industry is certainly a strong one and with the anticipated growth, reaching the number two position by next year is certainly plausible.

As we discussed, I am extremely confident that I can make a substantial contribution to your strategic development efforts based on my past accomplishments:

- Seven years' experience in B2B environment with Fortune 100 company, with three President Club wins based on my performance
- Developed strategic partnerships resulting in $106 million in revenue
- Managed B2C retail environment for two years and developed skill in hiring and training my team
- My district manager team had lowest turnover in division, as did my store manager team

Mr. Hannigan, there really is a mutual fit here. Together, I believe we can achieve Chase's objectives by next year. With the new points of presence Chase is planning, along with the depth of training, and my experience, we can lead Chase to that number two spot next year. Please expect a call from me this Friday to discuss the opportunity in more detail.

Sincerely,

Helen Kramer

Kris Mills
1 PR Way, Puerto Rico 00000 (487) 555-5555

April 2, 20__

Brenda Walsh
BW Securities
16111 Blue Ridge Circle
Palm Beach, FL 33440

Dear Ms. Walsh:

Thanks for meeting with me on Tuesday to speak about your physical therapist opportunity. I was especially intrigued by our discussion of alternatives to surgery via rehabilitation. Given the emphasis on rehabilitation for the elderly, your firm's emphasis, this is an opportunity to put my academic training to work and really feel like I am helping those in need as well.

Since our meeting, I've been mulling over the locations we discussed and the challenges you described in this discipline within the rehabilitation opportunities. I do believe my patience and upbeat personality, along with my formal training, make me an ideal candidate.

I will give you a call Monday to discuss the opportunity in more detail and possible locations in Palm Beach County.

Sincerely,

Kris Mills

Patricia Arbor
I Castle Way, Fort Worth, TX 77777 817.555.1111

May 19, 20__

Mr. Ronald Reese
Georgia Investments
One Peachtree Center
Atlanta, GA 33333

Dear Mr. Reese,

Thank you for taking the time to discuss the investment broker position at Georgia Investments with me. After meeting with you and observing the company's operations, I am further convinced that my background and skills coincide well with your needs.

I really appreciate that you took so much time to familiarize me with GI. It is no wonder that you retain your employees for so long. I feel I could learn a great deal from you and would certainly enjoy working with you.

In addition to my qualifications and experience, I will bring a strong and committed work ethic and sound judgment to this position. With the many demands on your time, I am sure that you require people who can start off with a short ramp-up time and begin contributing very quickly, and I can do this.

I look forward to my next meeting with you, Mr. Reese. Again, thank you for your time and consideration. I will give you a call next week to set up a follow-up meeting and provide you with the references we discussed.

Sincerely,

Patricia Arbor

Denise Riley
I Castle Way, Fort Worth, TX 77777 817.555.1111

November 14, 20__

Michael Stone
Dallas Center for Children
Irving, TX 77777

Dear Mr. Stone:

Thank you so much for taking the time to interview me today for the social worker position.

I felt a wonderful rapport not only with you, but also with the whole DCC staff. I am more convinced than ever that I will fit in beautifully as a member of the team and contribute my skills and talents for the benefit of children who need that guidance and help to set their course for adulthood.

I can make myself available for any further discussions of my qualifications that may be needed and would love to come in to meet with you again to discuss some new questions I have about your approach.

I will contact you this week to see if we can set up a follow-up meeting for late next week.

Thanks again for your consideration!

Best regards,

Denise Riley

George Starr

1 PR Way, Puerto Rico 00000
(487) 555-5555

November 19, 20___

Marie Holdonton
PeteTrade Financial
16111 Blue Ridge Circle
Palm Beach, FL 33440

Dear Ms. Holdonton:

I'd like to thank you for the time you spent talking with me about the marketing-research analyst position at PeteTrade Financial. I am very excited about this position and convinced that my financial training, both academically and at my current firm, has more than prepared me for the opportunity we discussed.

I meant to mention during the interview that earlier this year I was certified within the WW9 space. While this is not really required at this time for this position, it may be a valuable certification in the future and demonstrates the knowledge and my intellectual aptitude, given the difficulty in passing this exam the first time. Please contact me if you have any questions about my ability with this program or about any of my other qualifications.

I sincerely believe this opportunity is a wonderful mutual fit. I look forward to hearing from you soon, and thanks once again for meeting with me.

Sincerely,

George Starr

To: Jason Keller

From: Laura Lilienthal

Date: July 19, 20__

Subject: Meeting Follow-up

Dear Mr. Keller:

Thank you for the time you took to meet with me and discuss the project manager opportunity at Columbia Healthcare.

During our interview you mentioned two key characteristics you're looking for in your project manager. I know you expressed some concern in our meeting that I have not worked in the health-care industry before. I want to stress, however, that I am extremely well versed in the project management discipline and the transferable skills within it.

As for your requirement for industry experience, when I entered the public sector to work in project management, I was an outsider to that industry as well. Within just weeks I picked up on the industry nuances and within six months was the strongest project manager on staff.

I discovered, and I truly believe, that the inherent capabilities a strong candidate possesses can offset any weaknesses and be transferred much more easily than those of a weaker player with same-industry experience.

Thanks again, Ms. Lilienthal, for this wonderful opportunity to interview for the project manager position. I promise you I won't let you down if you give me the chance to show what I can do. I eagerly await the next step in the process.

Sincerely,

Laura Lilienthal

To: Sally Degner

From: John Canther

Date: October 13, 20__

Subject: Follow-up to Interview

Sally, I enjoyed speaking with you today about the account executive position at RCA Pharmaceutical and Medical. This position represents a strong mutual fit and is an excellent match for my skills and accomplishments. The creative approach to account management that you described confirmed my desire to work with you.

In addition to my strategic sales and presentation skills, I will bring to the position strong closing skills, initiative, and a history of winning at the top-tier sales level.

Thank you so much for the time you took to meet with me. I am very interested in working with RCA and look forward to hearing from you regarding this position.

Sincerely,

John Canther

To: Nathan Jackson

From: Chris Dupree

Date: May 14, 20___

Subject: Meeting Follow-up

Nathan, thank you for spending so much time with me yesterday. I really enjoyed discussing the direction in which Learning International is heading and your outlook for the next two to three years.

I did mean to mention that in addition to the training and delivery experiences I have had, I was the content developer for a training class called Interpersonal Management Skills, a four-module course to enhance a manager's coaching ability.

I appreciate your taking the time to meet with me once again and look forward to hearing from you in the coming days.

Chris

To: Mary Beth Burke

From: Jack Forger

Date: January 27, 20__

Subject: Follow-up to Interview

Mary Beth, thank you for considering me for the director of IT role with General Food Technologies. Though I was not selected, I sincerely appreciate the time you and your colleagues spent with me throughout the interview process.

You did mention you knew of a potential opportunity in the other consumer products organization. Would you mind helping me make a personal connection with that group?

I will call you in a few days and follow up with you. Thanks again for the your efforts and consideration. I'm looking forward to speaking with you soon.

Jack

To: John Eggman

From: Paul Walrus

Date: January 27, 20__

Subject: Follow-up to Interview

Thank you for interviewing me for the enterprise sales manager position. My experience as a sales leader in the Fortune 500 arena, and my success in penetrating these accounts, would make me a terrific complement to your organization. I'd also like to highlight my top skills:

Corporate Accounts
Dealing with up to 35 enterprise-level accounts on a daily basis, requiring strong account development skills and relationship building at the CxO level.

New Account Development
Managing my business, I cultivated new accounts and have a proven history of success in implementing marketing programs and meeting revenue quotas.

Closing
Moving from relationship development to closing key wins for ABC, the product penetration in my target market segment has been higher than that of any other enterprise sales leader in my organization. You mentioned that processing of computerized accounts was extremely important. Using computerized systems for the past four years; I have successfully integrated dozens of new systems and conversions.

Thanks once again for speaking with me, and I look forward to our next meeting. Please contact me at (214) 555-0000 if you have any questions.

Paul Walrus

To: Richard Youngston

From: Pamela Johnson

Date: September 20, 20___

Subject: Next Steps

Richard, I very much enjoyed having the opportunity to meet you and tour the PepsiCo campus this week. Thank you so much for taking the time to show me around and answer a few questions. Your facility impressed me as a warm, caring place for families to bring their loved ones and a pleasant working environment for employees.

I am very interested in continuing the process for the segment manager position we discussed. I have had more than seven years of experience in best-in-class brands of consumer products. I have worked very closely with the sales organizations, marketing, and brand management, as well as with Cirus Day, the leading advertising agency in the industry.

Attached is a brief plan of what I would do in my first ninety days on the job, and some personal performance accomplishments to support that I can accomplish what needs to be done. I'd love to discuss this with you later this week.

Sincerely,

Pamela Johnson

Pam Goodwin
3 Dragon Way, West Palm Beach, FL 33409

Salary History

2004 to present	Arcadia Resources		
	Vice President, Sales	*salary*	$125,000
		performance bonus	$ 50,000
	Regional Director	*salary*	$105,000
		performance bonus	$ 42,500
1997 to 2003	HCA		
	Lead Administrator	*salary*	$80,000
	Patient Support Manager	*salary*	$52,000
		incentive	$ 3,000
1993 to 1997	Columbia Healthcare		
	Business Manager	*salary*	$40,000

Note: Salary levels represent final compensation levels at end of period.

Linda Conner

111 Wylie Street, Danachestnut, TN 00000

Salary History

Company	Title	Total Compensation (salary plus bonus at plan)	
QQQ Financial	**Vice President of International Sales** 2005 to Present	Beginning: Ending:	$174,000 $189,000
Ferdinand Yost Foundation	**Director of Sales** 1999 to 2005	Beginning: Ending:	$112,000 $147,000
Nelson & Briggs Company	**Senior Account Executive** 1994 to 1999	Beginning: Ending:	$62,000 $96,000
Oneclick Directories	**Senior Account Manager – Commercial Systems Group** 1988 to 1994	Beginning: Ending:	$42,000 $58,000

15

References and Complimentary Letters

When you have your network of contacts in place, one of your strategies will be to ask for and work on personal/professional referrals. A referral cover letter introduces a candidate and his/her credentials based on a formal or informal introduction from a third party.

The most effective way to utilize the referral process is to ask the party referring you to make the formal introduction himself/herself. In other words, if a close former colleague knows the head of recruiting, then ask your friend to endorse your candidacy for employment and inform the recruiter that you will be calling on her or sending her a resume.

A couple years ago I was interviewing an internal candidate for a general manager position. While in the interview, I expressed two concerns or discussion points, though they were not deal breakers. One concern was this candidate's ability to work cross-functionally, across multiple disciplines; the other was his multichannel sales experience.

In the immediate wake of our interview, I received six phone calls and e-mails from various people this candidate had hand-picked. The unique thing about this orchestration was that each reference hit on a specific area or subject the candidate and I had discussed in the interview. I hired him for three reasons:

1. He had clearly made friendly contacts within the organization cross-functionally.

2. His references did address the concerns I had, and effectively at that.

3. For the candidate to go through that much effort, he must have really wanted the job and been hungry to achieve.

Here are some examples of people you might select for your references:

- Former managers can, of course, speak on your performance. This is the ideal reference.
- Peers are also good because they can talk about your performance and ability to work as a team member.
- In the spirit of a 360 reference, subordinates or direct reports may be better than peers. They can speak of your management style and ability to lead and motivate.
- Clients/customers/vendors/partners are also very good in the spirit of a 360-type of reference. Be certain to check with them first, in case you believe or expect them to give you a great reference but they are unwilling when you really need them to do so.

Many people leave a job and sever all ties with their colleagues. I hate writing an overused cliché, but *do not burn bridges*! Regardless of how you leave, you must allow yourself the option to approach people for references. If you make a concerted and genuine effort, most former managers, peers, and direct reports will support you with a great reference. Always be gracious and grateful, with sincerity for others' help. And when called upon on behalf of other colleagues, go out of your way to help them if they have earned it. Here are a few tips to manage the reference process:

- Prepare your reference list in advance.
- Alert your references that they might be contacted.
- Manage them—script them, if they are willing, on what to specifically address.
- If the reference is going to be in writing, ask to see it before, or even after, it is sent out. However, do not have yourself copied on the e-mail.
- Send a thank-you note/e-mail to the people who provided a reference.

To: Patricia Capizza

From: Lauren Arbit

Date: August 19, 20__

Subject: Thanks!

I want you to know that we are very pleased with the quality of work you have exhibited this past year. I sincerely appreciate your responsiveness and the way you conduct business. I have recommended you for a promotion and look forward to working with you for years to come.

You have done a wonderful job of supporting my group and our needs as we launched our new offering this year. I can't remember a time when we were so well supported by another group within the company, always with a smile and always with great follow-through and attention to detail.

Specifically, thanks, too, for the computer benchmarks produced to help us measure our progress; they really are excellent! Computer benchmarks produced by an independent third party in your group provide a professional and unbiased standard that the industry relies on for making critical purchasing decisions. Thank you once again for your contribution to the company and specifically my group.

Lauren

181—COMPLIMENTARY MESSAGE

To: Rhamid Ghalds

From: Atish Mroudle

Date: April 4, 20__

Subject: We Could Not Have Done It Without You

I hope you've had a chance to look at our recent sales performance. It is very impressive. I am proud of both your individual and your collective contributions to our sales effort. This is a very exciting time to be working in this industry, with an opportunity for us to make a difference in the marketplace. Keep up the good work.

Please convey these compliments to your entire staff for exceeding their goals for the last quarter of this year. It was truly a commendable performance. I know these things do not happen without a great deal of effort on the part of everyone, and I want you to know how much we appreciate your hard work. It appears that your emphasis on regular training sessions has paid dividends. Keep up the good work. We are proud of our entire team.

Specifically, I want to mention the training support you provided: instructor-led training in the conference room and in the field really made a difference. Paula Taylor was exceptional in her contribution to teaching better closing techniques and in getting the teams to tighten up their sales presentations.

I notice that customers and other salespeople defer to you when they need expert information on our sports apparel. I am pleased that you are so knowledgeable. I recognize the effort it takes to keep abreast of new developments and commend you for your good work. We are pleased that you enjoy working at Galyans.

Thanks again,

Atish

To: Kevin Alcorn

From: Codie Carly

Date: June 28, 20__

Subject: Congratulations!

Congratulations! Your work group achieved the highest-quality production of the whole factory last month. In addition to having the highest overall score, your group also had the lowest rework percentages in the plant. This is particularly impressive, since our overall quality figures were up for all departments for the month.

I want to remind each chairperson that our fund-raising deadline is approaching rapidly and we are still short of our goal. You have all been remarkably effective in getting the support of your groups and I am sure we can reach our goal this week if we all give one more push. What a great feeling it will be to accomplish what seemed impossible six months ago. You are setting new standards. Let's finish the job right and then celebrate!

Kevin, we are well aware of your personal contributions to the Siphion project. Given a complex problem, you have a rare and enviable ability to find a simple solution. It is delightful to see how your eyes light up when you are working on new ideas. Thank you for the enthusiasm you add to the team. You are a great contributor. We hope you will be inspiring us with your innovative thinking for years to come.

I want to compliment you on getting the sales brochure out in record time. I know you had to spend time on Saturdays to pull things together after some of the data was lost, but you did it without complaint. I trust these kinds of pressures will be a thing of the past as we get new equipment. We sincerely appreciate your outstanding work in getting this campaign started right. Thank you, again, for taking this problem in stride. You have a promising future in the company.

Codie

To: Steven Miller

From: Brian McIntee

Date: November 11, 20__

Subject: Bob Dailey

Mr. Miller, please accept this e-mail as a letter of recommendation for Bob Dailey.

Bob worked for me for the past year and I found him to be a strong contributor to the organization. When he took over, the team he inherited really needed an overhaul and several of the people needed to be replaced. He did that, and definitely left a stronger team than he inherited.

His position was eliminated, and the circumstances causing him to lose his position had nothing to do with his performance. I would hire him all over again, and had he not lived in the market he did, he would not have lost his position.

I am fully recommending him, and welcome your call should you have any questions.

Brian McIntee

Director of Operations

305-555-0000

To: Stacey Buck

From: Gillian Barr

Date: August 23, 20__

Subject: Pam Starwy

Ms. Buck, I understand you are considering Pam Starwy for a position within your company. You would be fortunate to have Pam on board. We definitely benefited from Pam's expertise in staffing, performance management, and employee and customer relations.

Her management style helped us grow more than 40%, year over year, for two years running, in a flat market. She did a wonderful job of building strong fundamentals in her team, and when she resigned to move out of state we saw that her impact was long lasting.

Her skill in anticipating changing technologies resulted in contributions to net profits in the millions of dollars during her last couple years with us.

We sincerely tried to retain her when she told us she was moving, but it just was not able to come together.

Stacey, feel free to contact me with any questions you might have. I can assure you the experience we had with Pam was very positive and one I would repeat, given the chance.

Gillian Barr

Senior Vice President

770-555-0000

To: Bob Brasenlin

From: Peter Norton

Date: May 14, 20__

Subject: Walter Gordon

Mr. Brasenlin, please allow me to introduce myself. My name is Peter Norton and I am Walter Gordon's former manager. Walter worked for CES and reported to me for the past three years.

In that time, Walter built a team from scratch in our start-up environment. He managed up to sixteen stores for us, most recently fourteen in the Denver area. In his district, we had below-average turnover, above-average performance results, and consistent profits month after month.

Walter was also a solid contributor out of the box, helping to contribute constructively to the corporate direction taken and strategic shifts the business needed. He participated in a special group, an internal "think tank" of selective field managers to discuss corporate issues and help determine the course of action to take.

He was definitely a top performer for us, with a great attitude.

Feel free to contact me if you have any questions.

Peter Norton

Vice President, Operations

888-555-1111

Eileen Simon

1 Houston Drive, Houston, TX 77777 832.555.1111 ra@watg.org

August 1, 20__

Mr. Isaiah Wallace
Vice President, Limited Corporation
1 Dublin Drive
Dublin, OH 44444

Dear Isaiah:

Thank you so much for agreeing to be on my list of references. Your support when I recently applied for the marketing position at Comerica Bank was much appreciated and, frankly, successful. After your e-mail to Tracie Gusola, I interviewed for the position and have since been offered it. I accepted.

I appreciate your efforts on my behalf—sincerely I do. Please, let's keep in touch and let me know if there is ever anything I can do to reciprocate. I am so thankful that you were not simply a passive name on a sheet of paper but an active advocate and much-needed supporter of my efforts. Again, thank you.

Sincerely,

Eileen Simon

William Hoover

1 Plaza Space
Kansas City, KS 00000
(816) 555-0000

August 12, 20__

Mr. Paul Kramer
Director, The Store
1 Metcalf Place
Overland Park, KS 00000

Dear Paul:

I appreciate the kind letter of recommendation you wrote to support my job search efforts. Yesterday, I received an offer to begin work as the marketing director with P&G. Your support of my accomplishments and strengths made a difference in the process, and I am so very grateful. If there is anything I can do in return, please contact me. Thank you again.

Sincerely,

Bill

To: Paul O'Neal
From: Monty Deyo
Date: April 1, 20__
Subject: Thank You!

Paul:

I am happy to inform you that I have accepted an offer to become the accounts payable manager at Hearling Enterprises. I should begin work within the next weeks.

I would like to thank you for all your help over the past few months, specifically for putting me in touch with Bridgit Grayling at Hearling. If there is ever anything I can do in return, please don't hesitate to contact me. Yours was a favor I will not soon forget. Every time I spoke with you I was so encouraged I felt like running a marathon; you are a great colleague and inspiration. Again, many thanks and best wishes.

Sincerely,

Monty

16
Resignation Letters

When you have accepted a job offer while working for another employer, oftentimes a letter of resignation is in order. For the most part, these letters should be very brief in nature and show no animosity whatsoever. They should build on past successes shared between you and the company, as well as praise specific individuals.

There may be specific instances when you feel the need to be critical of some aspect of the past, but that is a professionally immature perspective. Please do not put anything in writing that might be negative. Industries are incredibly small circles, even nationwide, and you'll be amazed at how you will cross paths with the same people within an industry throughout your career.

Kevin Alcorn

1 King Arthur
Carrollton, TX 75555
(972) 555-5555

July 19, 20__

Ms. Diane Gallagher
Senior Manager, Client Enterprise Division
430 Houston Way
Houston, TX 78444

Dear Ms. Gallagher:

Regretfully, I am writing to decline your firm's generous employment offer. While I am very interested in your company and think that there is a mutual fit, I cannot relocate to Houston at this time.

I sincerely appreciate the time you and your team spent with me throughout the interview process as well as the field day spent to acquaint me with the business.

Diane, thank you again for your consideration. I am confident you will identify an appropriate candidate. Please offer my best regards to the management team at Halliburton.

Sincerely,

Kevin Alcorn

TAMMY SHANAHAN

1 Melbourne Way, Melbourne, FL 33333 321.555.1111 ts@qway.net

September 19, 20__

Mr. Steven Sherbin
Administrator, Melbourne Medical
1999 Eau Galllie, Melbourne, FL 33333

Dear Mr. Sherbin:

Thank you so much for the time you and your team took with me each step of the way throughout the interview process. Your team was very forthright in their commentary about the strengths and opportunities within MM and in setting proper expectations. I really appreciate the offer you sent me yesterday.

As we mentioned during each of our meetings, I have been in similar discussions with another hospital in Brevard County.

After a great deal of thoughtful consideration, I must respectfully decline your most generous offer. Thank you so much for the time you spent with me and your investment in the interview process. At this point in my career I believe it is in my best interest to accept the other position because it offers a more aggressive compensation plan.

I would like to stay in contact with you professionally since we are in the same industry and county. And I would still consider working with your team if the compensation package was closer to what I really need. I am certain we would have worked well together, and perhaps that will happen in the future. I wish you the best of luck in completing your search. Feel free to call on me anytime.

Sincerely,

Tammy Shanahan

Thomas Doherty

10 Franklin Drive, Franklin, TN 00000
(615) 555-5555

October 1, 20__

Tori Rewert
AER Development Inc.
1 Plaza Circle
Kansas City, MO 00000

Dear Ms. Rewert:

I appreciate your offer of employment as director of engineering at AER Development, Inc.

As you may remember from our conversation during my interview, I am most interested in the design and development of commercial structures. I really do like what you have developed in the residential arena, but my passion is drawn toward larger and more complex structures, even though the development cycle is longer.

I would like to thank you and the managers of the Engineering Department for the consideration shown to me throughout the interviewing process.

Sincerely,

Thomas Doherty

Lucille Moisan

14 Davison, Detroit, MI 48888 313.555.0000

May 1, 20__

Mr. Connor Carter
Sprint Communications Company Ltd.
21 Peachtree Street
Atlanta, GA 33333

Dear Mr. Carter:

Thank you for the offer of a position as an indirect account executive with Sprint. After extensively considering my job offers, I have chosen to accept a position with another company. It was a difficult decision because your offers were comparable and I liked both companies, but the accounts supported were the deciding factor.

Thanks again for all your consideration.

Sincerely,

Lucille Moisan

Doris Frontly

1 Von Karmon, Irvine, CA 99999
df@qqqr.com

March 14, 20__

Ms. Kristin North
Director of Recruiting, Pelican Hill
999 John Carpenter Freeway
Las Colinas, TX 72222

Dear Kristin:

Thank you very much for offering me the opportunity to work at Pelican Hill. Unfortunately, I will not be accepting the position, as it does not fit the path I am taking to achieve my career goals.

Once again, I'd like to express my gratitude for the offer and my regrets that it didn't work out. You have my best wishes in finding someone suitable for the position.

Sincerely,

Doris Frontly

Adrian Gonzalez

1 Strongbert Way   Stoneham, MA 00000   (508) 555-1111

January 26, 20__

Ms. Renee Powers
Senior Partner
Robert Half and Associates
1 Harbor Town
Boston, MA 00000

Dear Ms. Powers:

I spoke with you over the phone several weeks ago regarding the status of my application for the business manager position with AirTouch. While I understand that you are still in the process of providing clients and getting feedback on others, I wanted to notify you that I have just accepted an offer for a similar position. Therefore, I respectfully request that you remove my candidacy from consideration.

Thank you for the time you spent with me throughout the interview process. Perhaps someday we may cross paths, through either your firm helping me in a search of my own or a potential position for me in the future. Again, thank you for your consideration.

Sincerely yours,

Adrian Gonzalez

To:	Court Kaylor
From:	Steve Miller
Date:	July 18, 20__
Subject:	Staff Writer Position

Thank you for your offer of employment and for your confidence in my abilities as a potential writer to join the McGadden team. As I explained during our phone conversation, I have reevaluated the thought of relocating to Atlanta. After much deliberation, I have decided that I cannot relocate and will remain in Dallas. I regret to have to tell you that I must decline your offer.

I apologize for informing you by e-mail, but I wanted to let you know of my decision as soon as I could so you can continue your recruiting effort. I am very willing to discuss this decision if you like. I will give you a call tomorrow and if I can help you with the search for another candidate, I would be happy to do so.

I regret not being able to accept the opportunity to work with you. Again, I appreciate your offer. My interest was most sincere, and it is very difficult to now decline this great opportunity. Please convey my best to all whom I met during the interview process.

Steve

Tracie Russell
101 Waco Way, Waco TX 75555 tr@erc.org

September 23, 20__

Mr. Patrick Dudash
RTC Consumer Products, Inc.
1 Addison Drive
Addison, TX 75240

Dear Mr. Dudash:

I would like to thank you for the chance to interview for the human resources manager position at RTC. Although disappointed I was not chosen, I enjoyed meeting with you and your staff and learning more about your company.

I remain very interested in opportunities with RTC, and I would appreciate it if you would keep me in mind for future openings where you think there may be a mutual fit. Your thoughts regarding my potential to someday join you and your colleague are welcome as well.

I would also welcome consideration for freelance assignments in support of any special projects that might arise.

Thanks again for past and future consideration.

Sincerely,

Tracie Russell

Memo

To: Dawn McCarter
From: Daniel Leftignore
Date: 2/14/20___
Re: Partner Management Position

Dear Ms. McCarter:

Thank you so much for considering me as long-term partner manager. Working with you and your team, and continuing the work I have already done within this organization but in a capacity of partnering with you has been a very exciting opportunity.

I am disappointed I was not selected to continue in the organization in this role. You cited several reasons for not moving forward with me, which included what you termed a "lack of introspection with my current group" as well as "not recognizing the positive characteristics of my fellow team memember."

Having been a part of this organization for nearly a decade and having realized two previous promotions in this time, I was surprised.

I will take your suggestions and make every attempt to improve in these areas for my own development, whether a future opportunity with you exists or not. Thank you so much for all your time and inspiration, and I wish you and your group all the best in the future.

Daniel Leftignore

Mark Young
111 Wylie Street, Danachestnut, TN 00000

February 12, 20__

Ms. Tammy Cancela
Director of Marketing, Leap Communications
101 Dallas Street, Suite 600
Nashville, TN 00000

Dear Tammy:

As you requested, I am submitting this letter to you to serve as my official resignation from Leap Communications. My official date of resignation will be February 28, 20__.

You also asked me to document my reasons for leaving Leap. I have been on board for just over three years. I have enjoyed my tenure with the group and have learned many things. I hope I have materially contributed as well. In 2007 and 2008 I was awarded the Merit of Excellence award in marketing. Both awards were wonderful recognitions of what we accomplished in rolling out the wireless broadband initiative.

However, over the past two years, Leap has made commitments to me they have been unable to keep. I was passed over for a promotion in late 2007 and do not appear to be on a promotional track at this time. Considering my performance and lack of upward mobility, I am forced to consider other growth opportunities.

I sincerely appreciate all you and Leap have done for me and look forward to staying in touch with a team that has become my family.

Sincerely,

Mark Young

Jennifer Johnson

111 Thompson Street
New York, NY 00000

November 29, 20____

Ms. Michelle Bristow
District Manager, Victoria's Secret/Limited Brands, Inc.
1 Baltimore Way
Baltimore, MD 00000

Dear Michelle:

Please accept my resignation effective December 15 from my position as manager of the Victoria's Secret store 1111 at Towson Center Mall.

I have enjoyed my time with Limited Brands. I feel I have grown as a manager and am most proud of taking this store location from the middle level of performance in your district to the top.

As you know, I am expecting a child in early January. I have decided I will not return to work after my scheduled maternity leave next year.

I will be happy to provide a bridge from my management to that of a replacement, within reason. I appreciate all you and the company have done for me and do not want to leave you in a bind.

Thanks so much for your support during my time here, and please let me know by next week if you need me beyond my proposed resignation date.

Sincerely,

Jennifer Johnson

Scott Wilson
111 Anaheim Avenue, Los Angeles, CA 90200

March 6, 20__

Mr. Adrian Gonzalez
President, Alco Industries
18200 Von Karmon
Irvine, CA 90000

Dear Adrian:

Please accept this letter as follow-up to the verbal resignation I gave you this morning. According to my employment agreement, given that the merger with SAS did not materialize, I am able to exit the company with a preagreed settlement and severance package.

I am now exercising that option. A copy of the agreement sent to me by former Alco president John Groomes is enclosed with this letter. My severance package enables a continuance of my salary and benefits for a period of fourteen months.

I am planning for my last day to be this Friday, in two days. Considering the sensitivity of my role in the firm, I have no doubt the board will want me separated as soon as possible. I can remain at my position for up to three weeks, if you need me. However, based on past experience with executives leaving Alco, I am sure you would prefer a date closer to this Friday.

Should Alco resist my prearranged severance package, I am fully prepared to exercise legal counsel to secure the obligation coming to me. You indicated you would have to seek board approval for this. Given the written agreement I am supplying, I do not see why there would be any delay. However, I am sure we can work this out amicably.

Please let me know by Friday morning your preferred course of action.

Sincerely,

Scott Wilson

To: Sal Todaro

From: Doug Matheson

Date: August 12, 20___

Subject: Resignation

The purpose of this letter is to resign from my employment with REI. My last day will be August 30, as we discussed.

I wish you nothing but success going forward and will miss working with you and many of my coworkers and customers. My employment with REI has been an opportunity both to learn and to contribute. I will take many positive memories with me to my new employment.

Again, best wishes for a positive future. Please call on me if there is anything I can do to help ease the transfer of my work or to help train your new employee.

Regards,

Doug

To: Brian Joyner

From: Tim Burke

Date: April 1, 20__

Subject: Resignation

Brian:

I am writing to you today to officially tender my resignation from Xyler-Johnson, effective April 15.

I never thought I would ever leave such a great company as Xyler-Johnson, but when the opportunity arose for a promotional position with another industry leader, I had to take it. As you know, that has always been a long-term goal for me, and I simply had to take advantage of it.

I cannot say enough wonderful things about Xyler-Johnson, about all the people I've encountered in my years of service with the company, and especially about you and all the others on the team. Your leadership has taken us to new levels, and I have appreciated all your personal and professional advice over the years. It's my hope that we will stay in touch as I begin this new chapter in my life.

If you have any questions, please ask. Thanks again for everything.

Sincerely,

Tim

Appendix: Keywords to Know

ACTION VERBS

A

accelerated, acclimated, accompanied, accomplished, achieved, acquired, acted, activated, actuated, adapted, added, addressed, adhered, adjusted, administered, admitted, adopted, advanced, advertised, advised, advocated, aided, affected, allocated, altered, amended, amplified, analyzed, answered, anticipated, appointed, appraised, approached, approved, arbitrated, arranged, ascertained, assembled, assessed, assigned, assisted, attained, attracted, audited, authored, authorized, automated, awarded

B

balanced, broadened, budgeted, built

C

calculated, canvassed, capitalized, captured, cast, centralized, chaired, challenged, changed, channeled, charted, checked, circulated, clarified, classified, cleared, closed, coauthored, collaborated, collected, combined, commissioned, committed, communicated, compiled, completed, composed, computed, conceived, conceptualized, concluded, condensed, conducted, conferred, consolidated, constructed, consulted, contracted, contrasted, contributed, contrived, controlled, converted, convinced, coordinated, corrected, corresponded, counseled, counted, created, critiqued, cultivated

D

decentralized, decreased, deferred, defined, delegated, delivered, demonstrated, depreciated, described, designated, designed, determined, developed, devised, devoted, diagrammed, directed, disclosed, discounted, discovered, dispatched, displayed, dissembled, distinguished, distributed, diversified, divested, documented, doubled, drafted

E

earned, edited, effected, elected, eliminated, employed, enabled, encouraged, endorsed, enforced, engaged, engineered, enhanced, enlarged, entertained, established, estimated, evaluated, examined, exceeded, exchanged, executed, exercised, expanded, expedited, explained, exposed, extended, extracted, extrapolated

F

facilitated, familiarized, fashioned, fielded, figured, financed, focused, forecasted, formalized, formed, formulated, fortified, found, founded, framed, fulfilled, functioned, furnished

G

gained, gathered, gauged, gave, generated, governed, graded, granted, greeted, grouped, guided

H

handled, headed, hired, hosted

I

identified, illuminated, illustrated, implemented, improved, inaugurated, increased, incurred, indoctrinated, induced, influenced, informed, initiated, innovated, inspected, inspired, installed, instigated, instilled, instituted, instructed, insured, interfaced, interpreted, interviewed, introduced, invented, inventoried, invested, investigated, invited, involved, isolated, issued

J

joined, judged

L

launched, lectured, led, lightened, liquidated, litigated, lobbied, localized, located

M

maintained, managed, mapped, marketed, maximized, measured, mediated, merchandised, merged, met, minimized, modeled, moderated, modernized, modified, monitored, motivated, moved, multiplied

N

named, narrated, negotiated, noticed, nurtured

O

observed, obtained, offered, offset, opened, operated, orchestrated, ordered, organized, oriented, originated, overhauled, oversaw

P

paid, participated, passed, patterned, penalized, perceived, performed, permitted, persuaded, pinpointed, pioneered, placed, planned, polled, prepared, presented, preserved, prevented, priced, printed, prioritized, probed, processed, procured, produced, profiled, programmed, projected, promoted, prompted, proposed, proved, provided, publicized, published, purchased, pursued

Q

Qualified, quantified

R

raised, ranked, rated, reacted, read, received, recommended, reconciled, recorded, recovered, recruited, rectified, redesigned, reduced, referred, refined, regained, regulated, rehabilitated, reinforced, reinstated, rejected, related, remedied, remodeled, renegotiated, reorganized, repaired, replaced, reported, represented, requested, researched, resolved, responded, restored, restructured, resulted, retained, retrieved, revamped, revealed, reversed, reviewed, revised, revitalized, rewarded, routed

S

safeguarded, salvaged, saved, scheduled, screened, secured, segmented, selected, sent, separated, served, serviced, settled, shaped, shortened, showed, shrank, signed, simplified, sold, solved, spearheaded, specified, speculated, spoke, spread, stabilized, staffed, staged, standardized, steered, stimulated, strategized, streamlined, strengthened, stressed, structured, studied, submitted, substantiated, substituted, suggested, summarized, superseded, supervised, supplied, supported, surpassed, surveyed, synchronized, synthesized, systematized

T

tabulated, tailored, targeted, taught, terminated, tested, tightened, took, traced, traded, trained, transferred, transformed, translated, transported, traveled, treated, tripled

U

uncovered, undertook, unified, united, updated, upgraded, used, utilized

V

validated, valued, verified, viewed, visited

W

weighed, welcomed, widened, witnessed, won, worked, wrote

KEYWORDS BY PROFESSION:

Account Executive:
- market penetration
- negotiation
- presentations
- relationship building
- initiative development
- territory penetration
- competitive market analysis
- prospecting
- solution-based selling
- consultative selling
- client needs analysis

- lead generation
- sales and marketing
- new business planning and development

Accounting:
- account reconciliation
- accounts receivable
- banking
- budgeting
- data collection and analysis
- expense tracking
- mergers and acquisitions
- information systems
- payroll
- cost accounting
- project management
- tax
- auditing
- risk management
- credit and collections
- collections
- cost reduction, cost accounting
- profit and loss (P&L)
- certified public accountant (CPA)
- generally accepted accounting principles (GAAP)
- tax planning/guidelines

Administrative Assistant:
- computer skills
- word processing
- dictation
- transcription
- spreadsheets
- appointment management
- travel arrangements
- letter composition
- call screening
- office management
- petty cash
- presentation preparation
- professional appearance
- staff supervision
- project management

Architect:

- multistate architect license
- program definition
- construction estimating and management
- site and cost analysis
- presentation graphics
- feasibility studies
- drawings and models
- public architecture
- design finalist
- zoning and codes
- commercial and residential architecture
- manpower allocation
- preservation consultant
- multilingual fluency

Auditor:

- audit management
- audit controls
- asset and liability management
- tax audits
- corporate development
- public and corporate accounting
- cost avoidance
- cost reduction
- cost/benefit analysis
- due diligence
- financial audits
- financial controls
- internal/external controls
- profit and loss (P&L) analysis
- regulatory compliance auditing

Banking/Finance:

- branch operations
- bank compliance
- cash management
- business development
- relationship management
- customer relations services
- branch sales action plan
- sales goals
- performance management

- staff coaching
- deposit/loan production
- online banking
- merchant services
- community relations
- budgets
- staff scheduling/management
- consumer credit
- customer service strategies
- consumer banking programs
- investment management
- retail lending
- return on investment (ROI)
- return on equity (ROE)
- return on assets (ROA)
- securities management
- foreign exchange
- unsecured lending

Bank Teller:
- banking; bank teller
- safe deposit
- ATM processing
- vault operations
- foreign currency exchange
- audit examination
- transaction approval
- processed data retrieval
- accountability of transactions
- daily settlement sheet
- lockbox processing
- transaction banking
- reconciliation projects
- ancillary sales referrals
- reconnet software
- loan documentation
- back operations accounting
- branch automation banking

Brand Manager:
- brand management
- advertising
- campaign management
- multigenerational product plan

- marketing communications
- cross-functional product team
- trend identification/analysis
- competitive advantage
- pricing strategies
- service strategies
- purchasing/cost reduction initiatives
- market share
- relationship building
- product/market launch
- competitive intelligence
- market research
- product life cycle management
- cradle-to-grave product life cycle

Call Center Manager:
- telecommunications
- customer relations
- multisite operations management
- quality improvement
- network administration
- call center
- technology solutions
- total quality management (TQM)
- advanced technology
- reengineering
- continuous process improvement
- customer service
- productivity improvement
- cost reduction
- performance improvement
- low employee turnover
- customer retention

Career Counselor/Life Coach:
- career development
- job search coaching
- career assessment
- group facilitation
- national certified career counselor (NCCC)
- career services
- career planning
- business networking
- job development

- vocational counseling
- academic counseling
- employment preparation
- resumes/cover letters

Change/Reengineering Consultant:

- reengineering consultant
- strategic partnership
- competitive market positioning
- cost containment
- profit growth
- relationship management
- multi-industry experience
- customer-driven management
- start-up
- continuous process improvement
- corporate culture change
- contract negotiations
- corporate image
- efficiency improvement

Chief Financial Officer (CFO):

- financial strategies/analysis
- asset/liability management
- strategic planning
- profitability modeling/forecasting
- profit and loss (P&L) management/analysis
- financial statement preparation
- regulatory compliance
- capital/operating budgets
- cross-functional-leadership team
- financial restructuring
- margin improvement
- audit management
- policy development
- financial planning/controls
- return on assets (ROA)
- return on equity (ROE)
- return on investment (ROI)
- corporate tax planning
- regulatory affairs compliance

City Manager:

- planning
- zoning regulations

- local ordinances
- public services
- economic development
- annual budget
- community relations
- municipal operations
- city council
- media relations
- project management
- eminent domain
- neighborhood revitalization

Construction:
- commercial and residential construction
- planned use development (PUD)
- project scheduling
- construction quality control management
- contracts and specification requirements
- construction safety
- soils and foundations
- cost estimating and competitive bidding
- crew and subcontractor supervision
- surveying
- concrete and steel design
- plumbing, HVAC, electrical
- general contractor
- remodeling/build-outs
- new construction
- restoration
- renovation
- rough/finish carpentry
- subcontractors

Corporate Attorney:
- corporate law
- in-house counsel
- corporate policy manuals
- mergers and acquisitions
- joint ventures
- venture capital
- employment law
- employee benefits plans
- contract negotiations
- business contracts

- trade regulations
- advertising and promotional law
- food and drug law
- product liability
- vendor agreements
- customer service agreements
- trademark rights

Corporate Recruiter:
- candidate screening
- standardized interviewing forms
- offer negotiation
- job fair development
- on-campus recruiting
- diversity training
- turnover—minimize or reduction
- skill assessment
- applicant tracking
- labor cost reduction
- affirmative action/equal employment opportunity (EEO)
- online recruiting
- human resources

Customer Service Representative:
- communication skills
- computer literate
- call center
- ACD
- MS Office skills

Dental Hygienist:
- oral examination
- orthodontics
- prosthetics and restorations
- teeth whitening
- oral hygiene and plaque control
- emergency treatment
- health record management
- billing and insurance
- appointment scheduling
- emergency treatment
- casts and impressions
- oral surgery and extractions
- instrument sterilization

Appendix: Keywords to Know

Editor:

- publicity
- advertising communications
- corporate communications
- electronic media
- corporate vision
- creative services
- customer communications
- marketing communications
- publicity
- public relations
- publishing houses

Engineering:

- design
- research
- manufacturing
- analog circuits
- digital circuits
- microprocessor
- power supply
- cap and cell construction
- bids and negotiation
- feasibility studies
- proposal development
- surveys and mapping
- networking
- telecommunications
- developing protocols
- prototypes
- ISO 9000
- calibration

Fund-raising:

- team leadership
- financial contributors
- revenue sources
- organizational development
- nonprofit institutions
- capital giving campaign
- organizational development
- direct-mail campaign
- board of directors
- grant writing

- policy development
- volunteer recruitment
- budgeting

Hospitality Industry:
- revenue management
- catering
- bar and beverage operations
- kitchen operations
- banqueting and conferences
- food production technology
- inventory cost control
- menu creation
- staff hiring and training
- purchasing vendor relations
- restaurant operations management
- guest services management
- convention coordinating
- front office management
- catering
- labor cost controls
- facilities planning

Human Resources:
- new-hire orientations
- personnel policies
- exempt and nonexempt employees
- Americans with Disabilities Act (ADA) regulations
- compensation programs
- cost per hire
- career paths
- training and development
- staffing/recruiting
- generalist
- human resources information system (HRIS)
- Consolidated Omnibus Budget Reconciliation Act (COBRA) administration
- benefits administration
- employee assistance programs
- manpower planning
- Equal Employment Opportunity (EEO) regulations
- organizational development
- performance appraisals
- salary structures

Insurance:

- insurance sales
- prospecting
- customer needs
- customer service
- repair versus replace
- claims
- adjustments
- coverage
- personal injury
- uninsured motorist/uninsured motorist property damage (UM/UMPD)
- site investigation
- estimating
- product introductions
- client base
- repeat business
- referrals

Journalism/Writing:

- writing skills
- creative
- interviewing
- nonfiction/fiction writing
- magazines and journals (specifics)
- business writing
- editing
- Web copy
- deadlines
- copyediting
- research skills
- newsletters

Loss Prevention:

- asset protection
- inventory shortage analysis
- electronic surveillance
- security operations
- industrial security
- stolen property
- store detectives
- undercover operations
- auditing
- security breaches
- employee integrity interviews

- policies and procedures
- revenue loss
- security reports
- informants
- internal theft investigations
- physical inventory
- shrinkage
- charge-backs
- fraud training

Manufacturing (Leadership):
- facilities consolidation
- technology integration
- cost reductions
- automated manufacturing
- outsourcing
- efficiency improvement
- inventory control
- value-added processes
- automated manufacturing
- union negotiations

Marketing:
- brand management
- product launch
- B2B and B2C
- marketing strategy
- marketing communications
- client and vendor relations
- creative
- focus groups
- pricing and finance development
- distribution channels
- promotional programs
- special events and planning
- direct mail
- database marketing
- presentations
- co-op programs

Network Engineer/Architect:
- local area network/wide area network (LAN/WAN)
- TCP/IP protocols
- UNIX

- routing protocols
- troubleshooting
- services
- circuit design
- client/server programming
- configuring, debugging, programming at network level
- MS Windows protocols
- network security
- Cisco Certified Network Associate (CCNA)
- firewalls
- circuit design
- integration
- network design
- installation

Nurse:
- registered nurse (RN)
- long-term care
- managed care
- health care
- case management
- prognosis
- in-residence care
- patient admissions and discharge
- treatment plans
- rehabilitation plans
- patient care plan
- problem solving
- clinical intervention
- diagnostic models
- minimum data set (MDS)
- resident assessment instrument (RAI)
- nursing home
- patient education
- life support monitoring equipment

Pharmaceuticals:
- clinical selling skills
- territory sales producer
- dispensing
- intravenous (IV) compounding
- billing
- prescription
- health physics

- sterile techniques
- order entry
- medical terminology
- customer needs assessment
- hospital territory sales
- therapeutic knowledge
- client relationship management
- managed care accounts
- product positioning
- pharmacy consultant
- medication dosages, adverse effects and labeling
- regimen review
- medication counseling
- patient profile systems
- chemical compounding
- record-keeping systems
- OBRA and VBRA 40 regulations

Physical Therapist:
- injury prevention
- workplace wellness education
- progress charting
- strength analysis
- functional capacity
- activities of daily living (ADLs)
- rehabilitation services
- hydrotherapy
- respiratory efficiency
- injury management
- treatment planning
- assistive technology and supportive devices
- human anatomy and physiology
- range of motion
- uniform standards of patient care

Purchasing:
- contract negotiations
- competitive bidding
- acquisition management
- contract administration
- request for proposal (RFP)
- request for information (RFI)
- enterprise resource planning (ERP)
- Supply chain management (SCM)

- just-in-time (JIT) purchasing
- outsourcing
- proposal review

Sales:
- account development
- account management
- account retention
- competitive analysis
- consultative sales
- customer loyalty
- customer satisfaction
- direct sales
- indirect sales
- global markets
- multichannel distribution
- negotiations
- sales closing
- solutions selling
- revenue growth
- profit growth
- prospecting
- presentation skills
- networking
- overcoming objections
- territory management
- opening up new territory
- market penetration
- cold-calling
- customer relationship building
- alliance building

Senior Sales Manager/VP:
- market and product evaluation strategy
- C-level relationship building and negotiations
- multichannel distribution
- multiteam sales management
- solutions-based sales
- cross-functional teaming
- speed-to-market strategies
- strategic planning
- sales budgets
- competitive analysis
- sales force motivation and training

- sales program development
- national accounts
- enterprise accounts
- account planning
- consultative sales

Teaching:
- team teaching
- self-esteem
- intensive phonics
- literature-based reading
- Internet/computer learning games
- performance-based
- positive reinforcement
- tutoring
- learning centers
- hands-on learning
- developing themes across the curriculum
- student advocate
- assertive discipline
- counseling
- educational programs
- committee leadership
- parent and family relationships
- power writing;
- process learning; process writing
- continuing education
- classroom management
- mentoring
- role playing
- thematic units

Index